The Wiersbe
BIBLE STUDY SERIES

The
Wiersbe
BIBLE STUDY SERIES

REVELATION

In Christ

You Are an

Overcomer

DAVID C COOK

transforming lives together

THE WIERSBE BIBLE STUDY SERIES: REVELATION
Published by David C Cook
4050 Lee Vance Drive
Colorado Springs, CO 80918 U.S.A.

Integrity Music Limited, a Division of David C Cook
Brighton, East Sussex BN1 2RE, England

The graphic circle C logo is a registered trademark of David C Cook.

ISBN 978-1-4347-0231-9
eISBN 978-1-4347-0318-7

© 2011 Warren W. Wiersbe

The Team: Steve Parolini, Karen Lee-Thorp, Amy Kiechlin,
Sarah Schultz, Jack Campbell, Karen Athen
Series Cover Design: John Hamilton Design
Cover Photo: Veer

Printed in the United States of America
First Edition 2011

12 13 14 15 16 17 18 19 20 21

022321

Contents

Introduction to Revelation

The Main Message

The book of the Revelation of Jesus Christ has challenged and fascinated Bible students for centuries. In my own library, I have dozens of commentaries on this book, and no two authors completely agree on everything.

But this is not important. What is important is that we not miss the major message of Revelation: the glorious victory of Jesus Christ over all His enemies. It would be unfortunate for the Bible student to get so lost in the details of this stirring prophecy that he miss its tremendous and overarching truth that in Jesus Christ, we are overcomers!

Eternal Promises

John wrote this book to encourage first-century Christians who were experiencing great suffering. In every age of the church, Revelation has brought comfort and hope. Why? Because its symbols are timeless and may be understood by believers in any period of history; because its promises are eternal and may be trusted by all saints.

I believe that John prophesied about specific events and a specific sequence of events, but I do not want my personal interpretation of prophecy to deter you from understanding the main message of the book: Jesus Christ is the Conqueror, and all believers share in His great victory.

Unveiling

The word translated "revelation" simply means "unveiling." It gives us our English word *apocalypse,* which, unfortunately, is today a synonym for chaos and catastrophe. The verb simply means "to uncover, to reveal, to make manifest." In this book, the Holy Spirit pulls back the curtain and gives us the privilege of seeing the glorified Christ in heaven and the fulfillment of His sovereign purposes in the world.

In other words, Revelation is an open book in which God reveals His plans and purposes to His church. When Daniel finished writing his prophecy, he was instructed to "shut up the words, and seal the book" (Dan. 12:4 KJV); but John was given opposite instructions: "Seal not the sayings of the prophecy of this book" (Rev. 22:10 KJV). Why? Since Calvary, the resurrection, and the coming of the Holy Spirit, God has ushered in the "last days" (Heb. 1:1–2 KJV) and is fulfilling His hidden purposes in this world. "The time is at hand" (Rev. 1:3; 22:10 KJV).

John's prophecy is primarily the revelation of Jesus Christ, not the revelation of future events. You must not divorce the Person from the prophecy, for without the Person there could be no fulfillment of the prophecy. "He is not incidental to its action," wrote Dr. Merrill Tenney. "He is its chief Subject." In Revelation 1—3, Christ is seen as the exalted Priest-King ministering to the churches. In Revelation 4—5, He is seen in heaven as the glorified Lamb of God, reigning on the throne. In Revelation 6—18, Christ is the Judge of all the earth; and in Revelation 19, He returns to earth as the conquering King of

Kings. The book closes with the heavenly Bridegroom ushering His bride, the church, into the glorious heavenly city.

Whatever you do as you study this book, get to know your Savior better.

—Warren W. Wiersbe

How to Use This Study

This study is designed for both individual and small-group use. We've divided it into eight lessons—each references one or more chapters in Warren W. Wiersbe's commentary *Be Victorious* (second edition, David C Cook, 2008). While reading *Be Victorious* is not a prerequisite for going through this study, the additional insights and background Wiersbe offers can greatly enhance your study experience.

The Getting Started questions at the beginning of each lesson offer you an opportunity to record your first thoughts and reactions to the study text. This is an important step in the study process as those "first impressions" often include clues about what it is your heart is longing to discover.

The bulk of the study is found in the Going Deeper questions. These dive into the Bible text and, along with helpful excerpts from Wiersbe's commentary, help you examine not only the original context and meaning of the verses but also modern application.

Looking Inward narrows the focus down to your personal story. These intimate questions can be a bit uncomfortable at times, but don't shy away from honesty here. This is where you are asked to stand before the mirror of God's Word and look closely at what you see. It's the place to take a good look at yourself in light of the lesson and search for ways in which you can grow in faith.

Going Forward is the place where you can commit to paper those things you want or need to do in order to better live out the discoveries you made in the Looking Inward section. Don't skip or skim through this. Take the time to really consider what practical steps you might take to move closer to Christ. Then share your thoughts with a trusted friend who can act as an encourager and accountability partner.

Finally, there is a brief Seeking Help section to close the lesson. This is a reminder for you to invite God into your spiritual-growth process. If you choose to write out a prayer in this section, come back to it as you work through the lesson and continue to seek the Holy Spirit's guidance as you discover God's will for your life.

Tips for Small Groups

A small group is a dynamic thing. One week it might seem like a group of close-knit friends. The next it might seem more like a group of uncomfortable strangers. A small-group leader's role is to read these subtle changes and adjust the tone of the discussion accordingly.

Small groups need to be safe places for people to talk openly. It is through shared wrestling with difficult life issues that some of the greatest personal growth is discovered. But in order for the group to feel safe, participants need to know it's okay *not* to share sometimes. Always invite honest disclosure, but never force someone to speak if he or she isn't comfortable doing so. (A savvy leader will follow up later with a group member who isn't comfortable sharing in a group setting to see if a one-on-one discussion is more appropriate.)

Have volunteers take turns reading excerpts from Scripture or from the commentary. The more each person is involved even in the mundane tasks, the more they'll feel comfortable opening up in more meaningful ways.

The leader should watch the clock and keep the discussion moving. Sometimes there may be more Going Deeper questions than your group can cover in your available time. If you've had a fruitful discussion, it's okay to move on without finishing everything. And if you think the group is getting bogged down on a question or has taken off on a tangent, you can simply say, "Let's go on to question 5." Be sure to save at least ten to fifteen minutes for the Going Forward questions.

Finally, soak your group meetings in prayer—before you begin, during as needed, and always at the end of your time together.

Unveiling
(REVELATION 1)

Before you begin …
- *Pray for the Holy Spirit to reveal truth and wisdom as you go through this lesson.*
- *Read Revelation 1. This lesson references chapter 1 in* Be Victorious. *It will be helpful for you to have your Bible and a copy of the commentary available as you work through this lesson.*

Getting Started

From the Commentary

While the book of Revelation was originally sent to seven actual local churches in Asia Minor, John makes it clear that *any* believer may read and profit from it (Rev. 1:3). In fact, God promised a special blessing to the one who would read the book and obey its message. (The verb *read* means "to read out loud." Revelation was first read aloud in local church meetings.) The apostle Paul had sent letters to seven churches—Rome, Corinth, Galatia,

Ephesus, Philippi, Colossae, and Thessalonica—and now John sent one book to seven different churches. Early in the book, he had a special message from Christ to each church.

—*Be Victorious*, pages 20–21

1. Based on your initial reaction to Revelation, what was the purpose of John's book? What are some ways it might have been speaking to immediate circumstances? To future concerns? What are some of the key themes in Revelation?

More to Consider: It is worth noting that there are seven "beatitudes" in Revelation: 1:3; 14:13; 16:15; 19:9; 20:6; 22:7, 14. What is significant about the number seven in this instance and elsewhere in Scripture?

2. Choose one verse or phrase from Revelation 1 that stands out to you. This could be something you're intrigued by, something that makes you uncomfortable, something that puzzles you, something that resonates with you, or just something you want to examine further. Write that here.

Going Deeper

From the Commentary

"If you don't stop writing books," a friend said to me, "you will run out of people to dedicate them to!" I appreciated the compliment, but I did not agree with the sentiment. John had no problem knowing to whom his book should be dedicated! But before he wrote the dedication, he reminded his readers that it was the Triune God who had saved them and would keep them as they faced the fiery trials of suffering.

God the Father is described as the Eternal One (see Rev. 1:8; 4:8). All history is part of His eternal plan, including the world's persecution of the church. Next, the Holy Spirit is seen in His fullness, for there are not seven spirits, but one. The reference here is probably to Isaiah 11:2.

Finally, Jesus Christ is seen in His threefold office as Prophet (faithful Witness), Priest (First-begotten from the dead), and King (Prince of the kings of the earth). *First-begotten* does not mean "the first one raised from the dead," but "the highest of those raised from the dead." *Firstborn* is a title of honor (see Rom. 8:29; Col. 1:15, 18).

But of the three Persons of the Trinity, it is to Jesus Christ alone that this book is dedicated.

—*Be Victorious*, pages 22–23

3. Why would John choose to dedicate this book to Jesus? What significance might this have to the intended audience? What significance might this have for believers today?

From the Commentary

> The overriding theme of the book of Revelation is the return of Jesus Christ to defeat all evil and to establish His reign. It is definitely a book of victory and His people are seen as "overcomers" (see Rev. 2:7, 11, 17, 26; 3:5, 12, 21; 12:11; 15:2; 21:7). In his first epistle, John also called God's people "overcomers" (1 John 2:13–14; 4:4; 5:4–5). Through eyes of unbelief, Jesus Christ and His church are defeated in this world, but through eyes of faith, He and His people are the true victors. As Peter Marshall once said, "It is better to fail in a cause that will ultimately succeed than to succeed in a cause that will ultimately fail."
>
> —*Be Victorious*, page 23

4. Why was a book of "victory" so important to the early Christians who were suffering persecution? How is this message applicable today? In what

ways were God's people "overcomers" during the time of the early church?
How are God's people overcomers today?

From the Commentary

> The titles given to God in Revelation 1:8 make it clear
> that He is certainly able to work out His divine purposes
> in human history. *Alpha* and *Omega* are the first and last
> letters of the Greek alphabet; so, God is at the beginning
> of all things and also at their end. He is the eternal God
> (see Rev. 1:4), unlimited by time. He is also the Almighty,
> able to do anything. *Almighty* is a key name for God in
> Revelation (Rev. 1:8; 4:8; 11:17; 15:3; 16:7, 14; 19:6, 15;
> 21:22).
>
> God the Father is called "Alpha and Omega" in Revelation
> 1:8 and 21:6, but the name also is applied to His Son
> (Rev. 1:11; 22:13).
>
> —*Be Victorious*, pages 24–25

5. Why were the names given to God so important to the early Christians?
How does applying the name "Alpha and Omega" (Rev. 1:8; 21:6) to Jesus

support the argument for the deity of Christ? (See also Isa. 41:4; 44:6; 48:12–13.) Why is establishing the deity of Christ important to John?

From the Commentary

This book was born out of John's profound spiritual experience while exiled on Patmos….

On the Lord's Day, John heard a trumpetlike voice behind him (Rev. 1:9–11). It was Jesus Christ speaking! As far as we know, the apostle had not heard his Lord's voice since Christ had returned to heaven more than sixty years before. The Lord commissioned John to write this book and to send it to the seven churches He had selected….

John saw a vision of the glorified Christ (vv. 12–16). Revelation 1:20 makes it clear that we must not interpret this vision literally, for it is made up of symbols. The seven lampstands represent the seven churches that would receive the book….

What John did (vv. 17–18) was predictable. He fell at the Lord's feet as though he were dead! And this is the apostle who leaned on Jesus' breast (John 13:23)! A vision

of the exalted Christ can only produce awe and fear (Dan.
10:7–9).

—*Be Victorious*, pages 25–26

6. What does it mean in Revelation 1:10 that John was "in the Spirit"?
What's the significance of the voice being compared to a trumpet? Why do
you think John recorded his reaction to hearing Jesus? What purpose does
his reaction serve for readers then and now?

From the Commentary

John was told not to seal the book (Rev. 22:10) because
God's people need the message it contains. Revelation
can be understood, despite the fact that it contains mys-
teries that may never be comprehended until we meet
at the throne of God. John sent the book to the seven
churches of Asia Minor with the expectation that, when
it was read aloud by the messengers, the listening saints
would understand enough of its truths so as to be greatly
encouraged in their own difficult situations.

—*Be Victorious*, page 28

7. Why is Revelation such a misunderstood (and perhaps misinterpreted) book? Is it possible to step into the shoes of the early churches that were the originally intended audience for this message? How does that help us understand what God's message was for them? For us today?

From the Commentary

> Revelation is a book filled with symbols. Biblical symbols are timeless in their message and limitless in their content. For instance, the symbol of "Babylon" originates in Genesis 10—11, and its meaning grows as you trace it through Scripture, climaxing with Revelation 17—18. The same is true of the symbols of "the Lamb" and "the bride." It is exciting to seek to penetrate deeper into the rich meanings that are conveyed by these symbols.
>
> —*Be Victorious*, page 28

8. Why would God choose to speak to His people through symbols instead of clear, certain language? What is the benefit of symbolic teaching? What are the challenges in understanding it? What are some other symbolic

messages in Scripture that can easily be misunderstood? How does struggling to understand difficult messages move us closer to God?

More to Consider: What John wrote about would "shortly come to pass" (Rev. 1:1 KJV) because "the time is at hand" (v. 3 KJV). (Note also Rev. 22:7, 10, 12, 20.) The word shortly does not mean "soon" or "immediately," but "quickly, swiftly." Why would this message of "quickly, swiftly" be significant to Christians suffering persecution? How might it comfort them? What are the dangers of interpreting this as "soon"? How do we know God didn't mean "soon" when He gave John this message? (See 2 Peter 3.)

From the Commentary

Revelation is a book of prophecy. This is definitely stated in Revelation 1:3; 22:7, 10, 18–19; note also 10:11. The letters to the seven churches of Asia Minor dealt with immediate needs in those assemblies, needs that are still with us in churches today, but the rest of the book is devoted almost entirely to prophetic revelations. It was by seeing the victorious Christ presented that the persecuted Christians found encouragement for their difficult task of witnessing. When you have assurance for the future, you have stability in the present. John himself was suffering under the hand of Rome (Rev. 1:9), so the book was born out of affliction.

—*Be Victorious*, page 28

9. How does knowing that Revelation is a prophetic book help us to understand its message for today? What kind of encouragement did these prophecies give to the early church? What encouragement does the book offer to us today?

From the Commentary

Revelation is the climax of the Bible. All that began in Genesis will be completed and fulfilled in keeping with God's sovereign will. He is "Alpha and Omega, the beginning and the ending" (Rev. 1:8). What God starts, He finishes!

But before visiting the throne room of heaven, we must pause to listen to "the Man among the lampstands" as He reveals the personal needs in our churches and in our own hearts. "He that hath an ear, let him hear what the Spirit saith unto the churches" (Rev. 2:7, 11, 17, 29)!

—Be Victorious, page 29

10. Why is Revelation a fitting "last book" for the Bible? How does the revelation given to John help to tie up the larger story of God's redemption of man? What implications does this book have for today's Christians and how they work out their salvation?

Looking Inward

Take a moment to reflect on all that you've explored thus far in this study of Revelation 1. Review your notes and answers and think about how each of these things matters in your life today.

Tips for Small Groups: To get the most out of this section, form pairs or trios and have group members take turns answering these questions. Be honest and as open as you can in this discussion, but most of all, be encouraging and supportive of others. Be sensitive to those who are going through particularly difficult times and don't press for people to speak if they're uncomfortable doing so.

11. What's your first thought when you hear that someone is going to be teaching from the book of Revelation? How do you typically respond to Scripture passages you don't fully understand? What role does faith play in your study of this book?

12. The main theme of Revelation is Jesus' role as "overcomer." How is this message applicable to your life today? What are some of the evils in this world that you can't wait for Jesus to defeat? How important is it to you that you fully understand how this is going to happen?

13. What do you like best about the Bible's use of symbols? What frustrates you about them? What are some of the symbols you have the

hardest time with? How can you benefit from the struggle to understand those symbols?

Going Forward

14. Think of one or two things that you have learned that you'd like to work on in the coming week. Remember that this is all about quality, not quantity. It's better to work on one specific area of life and do it well than to work on many and do poorly (or to be so overwhelmed that you simply don't try).

Do you want to better understand the meaning of the symbols in Revelation? Do you want to learn how to trust Jesus' role as "overcomer"? Be specific. Go back through Revelation 1 and put a star next to the phrase or verse that is most encouraging to you. Consider memorizing this verse.

Real-Life Application Ideas: Revelation speaks about Jesus' ultimate victory over evil. But we are also compelled by faith to be God's hands and feet to fight evil while we're still here on earth. Think about some of the evils you know that affect your family, your church, or your community. Then make a plan of attack for fighting those evils in practical ways.

Seeking Help

15. Write a prayer below (or simply pray one in silence), inviting God to work on your mind and heart in those areas you've previously noted. Be honest about your desires and fears.

Notes for Small Groups:

- *Look for ways to put into practice the things you wrote in the Going Forward section. Talk with other group members about your ideas and commit to being accountable to one another.*

- *During the coming week, ask the Holy Spirit to continue to reveal truth to you from what you've read and studied.*

- *Before you start the next lesson, read Revelation 2—3. For more in-depth lesson preparation, read chapters 2 and 3, "Christ and the Churches—Parts I and II," in* Be Victorious.

The Churches
(REVELATION 2—3)

Before you begin …

- *Pray for the Holy Spirit to reveal truth and wisdom as you go through this lesson.*
- *Read Revelation 2—3. This lesson references chapters 2 and 3 in* Be Victorious. *It will be helpful for you to have your Bible and a copy of the commentary available as you work through this lesson.*

Getting Started

From the Commentary

If you have ever moved to a new community and had to select a new church home, you know how difficult it is to examine and evaluate a church and its ministry. Imposing buildings may house dying or dead congregations, while modest structures might belong to virile assemblies on the march for the Lord. The church we think is "rich" may turn out to be poor in God's sight (Rev. 3:17), while the "poor" church is actually rich (Rev. 2:9).

Only the Head of the church, Jesus Christ, can accurately
inspect each church and know its true condition, because
He sees the internals, not only the externals (Rev. 2:23b).
In these special messages to the seven churches in Asia
Minor, the Lord gave each assembly an "X-ray" of its
condition. But He intended for *all* the churches to read
these messages and benefit from them. (Note the plural
"churches" in Rev. 2:7, 11, 17, 29; 3:6, 13, 22.)

—*Be Victorious,* page 33

1. Chapters 2 and 3 in Revelation address specific churches. What are some
of the messages God gave these churches? In what ways are these messages
also applicable to individuals?

2. Choose one verse or phrase from Revelation 2—3 that stands out to
you. This could be something you're intrigued by, something that makes
you uncomfortable, something that puzzles you, something that resonates
with you, or just something you want to examine further. Write that here.

More to Consider: John was a pastor at heart. What can you learn about his "pastor's heart" in the way he tries to encourage these churches in difficult times? What can today's pastors learn from the way John reached out?

Going Deeper

From the Commentary

> The Ephesian assembly had enjoyed some "stellar" leadership—Paul, Timothy, and the apostle John himself—but the Lord reminded them that *He* was in control of the ministry, placing the "stars" where He pleased. How easy it is for a church to become proud and forget that pastors and teachers are God's gifts (Eph. 4:11) who may be taken away at any time. Some churches need to be cautioned to worship the Lord and not their pastor!
>
> —*Be Victorious*, page 34

3. What does "you have forsaken your first love" mean (Rev. 2:4)? Why do churches forsake their first love? What warnings does this message to the Ephesian church have for us today? (See 2:1–7.)

From the Commentary

The church at Smyrna was not having an easy time of it! The members were persecuted, probably because they refused to compromise and say, "Caesar is Lord." Smyrna was an important center of the Roman imperial cult, and anyone refusing to acknowledge Caesar as Lord would certainly be excluded from the guilds. This would mean unemployment and poverty. The word used here for *poverty* means "abject poverty, possessing absolutely nothing."

A large Jewish community also thrived in Smyrna. The Jews, of course, did not have to patronize the imperial cult since their religion was accepted by Rome, but they certainly would not cooperate with the Christian faith. So, from both Jews and Gentiles, the Christians in Smyrna received slander and suffering.

But they were rich! They lived for eternal values that would never change, riches that could never be taken away. "As poor, yet making many rich" (2 Cor. 6:10; 8:9). In fact, their suffering for Christ only increased their riches.

Our struggles are not with flesh and blood, but with the enemy, Satan, who uses people to accomplish his purposes. The Jewish synagogue was actually a synagogue of Satan. A true Jew is not one physically or racially, but spiritually (Rom. 2:17–29).

—*Be Victorious*, pages 37–38

4. How might the message "be faithful, even to the point of death" have been received by the church in Smyrna? How would the promise of the "crown of life" have encouraged those who were suffering (Rev. 2:10)? What does it mean that our struggles are not with flesh and blood?

From the Commentary

Despite their courageous stand against persecution, the believers in Pergamos were not faultless before the Lord. Satan had not been able to destroy them by coming as the roaring lion (1 Peter 5:8), but he was making inroads as the deceiving serpent. A group of compromising people had infiltrated the church fellowship, and Jesus Christ hated their doctrines and their practices.

These infiltrators are called "Nicolaitans," whom we met already at Ephesus (Rev. 2:6). The name means "to rule the people." What they taught is called "the doctrine of Balaam" (Rev. 2:14). The Hebrew name *Balaam* also means "lord of the people" and is probably synonymous with *Nicolaitans*. Sadly, this group of professed believers "lorded it over" the people and led them astray.

—*Be Victorious*, page 39

5. Review the story of Balaam (Num. 22—24). Who was Balaam? How does this help us understand the false doctrine that the church in Pergamos was facing? What message does John give these Christians?

From the Commentary

The longest message was sent to the church in the smallest city! Thyatira was a military town as well as a commercial center with many trade guilds. Wherever guilds were found, idolatry and immorality—the two great enemies of the early church—were almost always present too.

The city boasted a special temple to Apollo, the "sun god," which explains why the Lord introduced Himself as "the Son of God" (the only time in Revelation this title is used). John had to deliver a message of severe warning and judgment to this congregation, which explains the description of the Lord's eyes and feet.

—*Be Victorious*, pages 41–42

6. In what ways was the church in Thyatira doing well (Rev. 2:19)? What were the accusations against the church (vv. 20–23)? What was the main thrust of John's message to this church (v. 25)?

From the Commentary

> The message to Sardis is a warning to all "great churches" that are living on past glory. Dr. Vance Havner has frequently reminded us that spiritual ministries often go through four stages: a man, a movement, a machine, and then a monument. Sardis was at the "monument" stage, but there was still hope!
>
> There was hope because Christ was the Head of the church and He was able to bring new life. He described Himself as the one possessing the seven Spirits and the seven stars. There is only one Holy Spirit (Eph. 4:4), but the number seven demonstrates fullness and completeness. The Holy Spirit gives life to the church, and life is exactly what the people at Sardis needed. The sevenfold Spirit of God is pictured as seven burning lamps (Rev. 4:5) and as seven all-seeing eyes (Rev. 5:6).

All of the church's man-made programs can never bring life, any more than a circus can resurrect a corpse. The church was born when the Spirit of God descended on the Day of Pentecost (Acts 2), and its life comes from the Spirit. When the Spirit is grieved, the church begins to lose life and power.

—*Be Victorious*, page 48

7. How would you describe the problem the church in Sardis was facing (Rev. 3:1–6)? How is that like or unlike problems facing today's church? What is the suggested solution for this church? What are practical ways a church can better live by the power of the Spirit in its ministry?

From the Commentary

The believers in Philadelphia were in a similar situation to that of Paul when he wrote 1 Corinthians 16:9—there were both opportunities and obstacles! Unbelief sees the obstacles, but faith sees the opportunities! And since the Lord holds the keys, He is in control of the outcome! So what do we have to fear? Nobody can close the doors as long as He keeps them open. Fear, unbelief, and delay have caused the church to miss many God-given opportunities.

The Savior gave three wonderful and encouraging promises to this church. First, He would take care of their enemies (Rev. 3:9)....

Second, He would keep them from tribulation (Rev. 3:10). This is surely a reference to the time of tribulation that John described in Revelation 6—19, "the time of Jacob's trouble." ...

The third promise to the Philadelphians is that God would honor them (Rev. 3:12). The symbolism in this verse would be especially meaningful to people who lived in constant danger of earthquakes: the stability of the pillar, no need to go out or to flee, a heavenly city that nothing could destroy.

—*Be Victorious*, pages 54–55

8. What protection from enemies does God promise the church in Philadelphia? What is the "open door" that is referenced in Revelation 3:8? Why is it a door that can't be shut? How does this offer encouragement? What is the open door that God has placed in front of today's church?

More to Consider: Philadelphia *means "love of the brethren." What is the biblical basis for the idea that brotherly love is an important mark of the Christian? (See John 13:34; Rom. 5:5; 1 Thess. 4:9; 1 John 4:19.)*

From the Commentary

As with some of the previous churches, the Lord adapted His words to something significant about the city in which the assembly was located. In this case, Laodicea was known for its wealth and its manufacture of a special eye salve, as well as of a glossy black wool cloth. It also was located near Hieropolis, where there were famous hot springs, and Colossae, known for its pure, cold water.

The Lord presented Himself as "the Amen," which is an Old Testament title for God (see Isa. 65:16, where the word *truth* is the Hebrew word *amen*). He is the truth and speaks the truth, because He is "the faithful and true Witness" (Rev. 3:14). The Lord was about to tell this church the truth about its spiritual condition; unfortunately, they would not believe His diagnosis.

"Why is it that new Christians create problems in the church?" a young pastor once asked me.

"They don't create problems," I replied. "They *reveal* them. The problems have always been there, but we've gotten used to them. New Christians are like children in the home: They tell the truth about things!"

The Laodicean church was blind to its own needs and unwilling to face the truth. Yet honesty is the beginning of true blessing, as we admit what we are, confess our sins, and receive from God all that we need. If we want God's best for our lives and churches, we must be honest with God and let God be honest with us.

—*Be Victorious*, pages 55–56

9. The message to the Laodicean church was that it was "neither cold nor hot." Why is it worse to be neither on fire for nor antagonistic toward God? What are the dangers for a lukewarm church? How does a church move out of this state?

From the Commentary

The letters to the seven churches are God's X-rays, given to us so that we might examine our own lives and ministries. Judgment is going to come to this world, but it first begins at God's house (1 Peter 4:17). In these letters we find encouragement as well as rebuke.

May the Lord help us to hear what the Spirit is saying *today* to the church, and to the individuals in the churches!

—*Be Victorious*, page 60

10. What sort of messages might God have given John to write about churches today (your church, for example)? How would these messages be similar to what is in Revelation? How can individuals discover the point of these messages for their own lives?

Looking Inward

Take a moment to reflect on all that you've explored thus far in this study of Revelation 2—3. Review your notes and answers and think about how each of these things matters in your life today.

Tips for Small Groups: To get the most out of this section, form pairs or trios and have group members take turns answering these questions. Be honest and as open as you can in this discussion, but most of all, be encouraging and supportive of others. Be sensitive to those who are going through particularly difficult times and don't press for people to speak if they're uncomfortable doing so.

11. How might you have felt as a member of one of the churches Jesus speaks to in Revelation 2—3? Are you more apt to respond to encouragement or correction? How do you react when you see something that's not right in your church?

12. Which church situation from Revelation 2—3 most closely matches your own today? Which issues most directly match those you're dealing with personally? How can these prophetic messages of encouragement and challenge help you overcome obstacles in your faith story?

13. In what ways have you been lukewarm like the Laodicean Christians? What are some things you can do to be hot in your love for God instead of lukewarm?

Going Forward

14. Think of one or two things that you have learned that you'd like to work on in the coming week. Remember that this is all about quality, not quantity. It's better to work on one specific area of life and do it well than to work on many and do poorly (or to be so overwhelmed that you simply don't try).

Do you want to overcome fear or unbelief as some of the churches had to do? Be specific. Go back through Revelation 2—3 and put a star next to the phrase or verse that is most encouraging to you. Consider memorizing this verse.

Real-Life Application Ideas: Invite leaders of your church to join you in a group discussion about the churches referenced in Revelation 2—3, with the primary purpose of examining your own church in light of what God has to say to each church. Look for ways you can practically build your church so it is a place free from contentious issues like those the early churches were facing. Use this time to better understand your church's goals and to refine them in a way that grows strong Christ-followers.

Seeking Help

15. Write a prayer below (or simply pray one in silence), inviting God to work on your mind and heart in those areas you've previously noted. Be honest about your desires and fears.

Notes for Small Groups:

- *Look for ways to put into practice the things you wrote in the Going Forward section. Talk with other group members about your ideas and commit to being accountable to one another.*

- *During the coming week, ask the Holy Spirit to continue to reveal truth to you from what you've read and studied.*

- *Before you start the next lesson, read Revelation 4—7. For more in-depth lesson preparation, read chapters 4 and 5, "Come, Let Us Adore Him!" and "The Seals and the Sealed," in* Be Victorious.

Worship and Wrath
(REVELATION 4—7)

Before you begin …
- *Pray for the Holy Spirit to reveal truth and wisdom as you go through this lesson.*
- *Read Revelation 4—7. This lesson references chapters 4 and 5 in Be Victorious. It will be helpful for you to have your Bible and a copy of the commentary available as you work through this lesson.*

Getting Started

From the Commentary

If Revelation 1:19 is God's inspired outline of this book, then Revelation 4 ushers us into the third division: "the things which shall be hereafter." In fact, that is exactly what God said to John when He summoned him to heaven! It would appear that, in this experience, John illustrates what will happen to God's people when the church age has run its course: Heaven will open; there will be a voice and the sound of a trumpet; and the saints will be caught up to heaven (1 Cor. 15:52; 1 Thess. 4:13–18). Then, God's judgment of the earth can begin.

—*Be Victorious,* page 63

1. Why do you think the book of Revelation takes such a dramatic turn in chapter 4? What purpose does this focus on the worship in heaven provide for believers? This section precedes one on God's wrath—on the things yet to come that aren't particularly pretty. Why would God show a glimpse of heaven first? How does this provide comfort for Christians who believe themselves to be in the "last times"?

More to Consider: The key word in chapter 4 is throne. In fact, this is a key word in the entire book of Revelation. Why do you think this word is used so frequently? What does this say about the importance of God's sovereignty? Why is that important to understand in light of the rest of Revelation?

2. Choose one verse or phrase from Revelation 4—7 that stands out to you. This could be something you're intrigued by, something that makes

you uncomfortable, something that puzzles you, something that resonates with you, or just something you want to examine further. Write that here.

Going Deeper

From the Commentary

> Whenever the living creatures glorified God, the elders would fall before the throne and praise Him. The book of Revelation is filled with hymns of praise (Rev. 4:8, 11; 5:9–13; 7:12–17; 11:15–18; 12:10–12; 15:3–4; 16:5–7; 18:2–8; 19:2–6). The emphasis on praise is significant when you remember that John wrote this book to encourage people who were going through suffering and persecution!
>
> —*Be Victorious*, pages 67–68

3. Review Revelation 4:9–11. What is the theme of this hymn? Why is creation mentioned in this passage? Why might God's role as Creator have been particularly important to the early Christians suffering persecution? Why focus on this attribute in this transitional section of Revelation?

From the Commentary

The focus of attention shifts in Revelation 5 to a seven-sealed scroll in the hand of God. The scroll could not be read because it was rolled up and sealed (like a Roman will) with seven seals. John could see writing on both sides of the scroll, which meant that nothing more could be added. What was written was completed and final.

The scroll represents Christ's "title deed" to all that the Father promised Him because of His sacrifice on the cross. "Ask of me, and I shall give thee the heathen [nations] for thine inheritance, and the uttermost parts of the earth for thy possession" (Ps. 2:8). Jesus Christ is the "Heir of all things" (Heb. 1:2). He is our beloved "Kinsman-Redeemer" who was willing to give His life to set us free from bondage and to restore our lost inheritance (see Lev. 25:23–46; the book of Ruth; Jer. 32:6–15).

As Christ removed the seals, various dramatic events took place. The seventh seal introduced the seven trumpet judgments (Rev. 8:1–2). Then, when the seventh trumpet had blown, the great day of God's wrath was announced, ushering in the "vial [bowl] judgments" that brought to a climax the wrath of God (Rev. 11:15ff.; 15:1). It is possible that the trumpet judgments were written on one side of the scroll and the bowl judgments on the other.

A title deed or will can be opened only by the appointed heir, and this is Jesus Christ. No one in all the universe could be found worthy enough to break the seals. No wonder John wept, for he realized that God's glorious redemption plan for mankind could never be completed until the scroll was opened.

—*Be Victorious*, page 69

4. Why is it significant that only Jesus can open the scroll (Rev. 5:3–10)? Why did this make John weep (v. 4)? What is significant about the symbolism of the slain lamb in this context?

From the Commentary

The worship experience in Revelation 5 offers us four reasons why we worship Jesus Christ.

(1) Because of who He is (vv. 5–7).

(2) Because of where He is (v. 6).

(3) Because of what He does (vv. 8–10).

(4) Because of what He has (vv. 11–14).

—*Be Victorious*, pages 69–73

5. Review the Scripture passages associated with the four reasons listed above. How does each of these passages support the reason noted? What does this entire section of Revelation teach us about worshipping Jesus?

From the Commentary

> The worship described in Revelation 4—5 is preparation for the wrath described in Revelation 6—19. It seems strange to us that worship and judgment should go together, but this is because we do not fully understand either the holiness of God or the sinfulness of man. Nor do we grasp the total picture of what God wants to accomplish and how the forces of evil have opposed Him. God is longsuffering, but eventually He must judge sin and vindicate His servants.
>
> According to Daniel 9, seven years are assigned to Israel in God's prophetic calendar, beginning with the signing of an agreement with the world dictator (the Antichrist), and ending with Christ's return to earth to judge evil and establish His kingdom. It is this period that is described in Revelation 6—19. By referring to John's outline (Rev. 1), you will see that his description is in three parts: the

first three and a half years (Rev. 6—9), the events at the middle of the period (Rev. 10—14), and the last three and a half years (Rev. 15—19).

—*Be Victorious*, page 77

6. Review Revelation 6—7. This is the beginning of a complex and much-examined portion of Revelation that has been the subject of disagreement and examination for centuries. As you look at these first two chapters, what stands out to you as being most significant? What is the point of the seals? The 144,000? Why might this section be so difficult to understand?

From the Commentary

In Revelation 6—7, John characterized the opening days of the tribulation as a time of retribution, response, and redemption.

In Revelation 6:1–8, John recorded the opening of the first four seals, and as each seal was opened, one of the four living creatures summoned a rider on a horse. ("Come and see" should read, "Come!") In other words, events take place on earth because of the sovereign direction of God in heaven.

The horse imagery is probably related to the vision described in Zechariah 1:7–17. Horses represent God's activity on earth, the forces He uses to accomplish His divine purposes. The center of His program is Israel, particularly the city of Jerusalem. (Jerusalem is mentioned thirty-nine times in Zechariah.) God has a covenant purpose for Israel, and that purpose will be fulfilled just as He promised.

Antichrist (vv. 1–2). Daniel states that there is a "prince that shall come," who will make a covenant with Israel to protect her from her enemies (Dan. 9:26–27). In other words, the future world dictator begins his career as a peacemaker! He will go from victory to victory and finally control the whole world.

War (vv. 3–4). The Antichrist's conquest begins in peace, but soon he exchanges the empty bow for a sword. The color red is often associated with terror and death: the red dragon (Rev. 12:3), the red beast (Rev. 17:3). It is a picture of wanton bloodshed....

Famine (vv. 5–6). The color black is often connected with famine (Jer. 14:1–2; Lam. 5:10). Famine and war go together. A shortage of food will always drive up prices and force the government to ration what is available....

Death (vv. 7–8). John saw two personages: Death riding a pale horse and hades (the realm of the dead) following him. Christ has the keys of death and hades (Rev. 1:18), and both will one day be cast into hell (Rev. 20:14). Death claims the body while hades claims the soul of the dead (Rev. 20:13). John saw these enemies going forth to claim their prey, armed with weapons of the sword, hunger, pestilence (death), and wild beasts.

—*Be Victorious*, pages 78–81

7. The four horses symbolize key elements that play key roles in this section of Revelation. Review Revelation 6:1–8 and note the interpretations suggested in the previous commentary excerpt. How do these interpretations help you understand the message of chapter 6? Why do you think these themes are important?

From the Commentary

John recorded two responses to the opening of the seals, one in heaven and the other on earth.

Verses 9–11 focus on the response of the martyrs. When the Old Testament priest presented an animal sacrifice, the victim's blood was poured out at the base of the brazen altar (Lev. 4:7, 18, 25, 30). In Old Testament imagery, blood represents life (Lev. 17:11). So, here in Revelation, the souls of the martyrs "under the altar" indicates that their lives were given sacrificially to the glory of God....

Verses 12–17 focus on the response of the earth-dwellers. The martyrs cried, "Avenge us!" but the unbelievers on earth will cry, "Hide us!" The opening of the sixth seal will produce worldwide convulsions and catastrophes, including the first of three great earthquakes (Rev. 6:12; 11:13; 16:18–19). All of nature will be affected: the sun, moon, and stars, as well as the heavens, the mountains, and the islands.

—*Be Victorious*, pages 81, 83

8. Read Philippians 2:17 and 2 Timothy 4:6. How is the message of these verses similar to the description of the martyrs' role in Revelation 6:9–11? Review Revelation 6:12–17. Now read Joel 2:30–31; 3:15; and Isaiah 13:9–10; 34:2–4. How does the scene in Revelation compare with these verses? Even without understanding the meaning of the symbolism, how might readers respond to these descriptions? Why do you suppose such a frightening picture is painted here?

More to Consider: Review Revelation 7. What are the two groups described here? Contrast and compare them. What stands out to you about the way they're described?

From the Commentary

> In Scripture, a seal indicates ownership and protection. Today, God's people are sealed by the Holy Spirit (Eph. 1:13–14). This is God's guarantee that we are saved and safe, and that He will one day take us to heaven. The 144,000 Jews will receive the Father's name as their seal (Rev. 14:1), in contrast to the "mark of the beast" that the Antichrist will give those who follow him (Rev. 13:17; 14:11; 16:2; 19:20).
>
> This seal will protect these chosen Jews from the judgments that will "hurt the earth and the sea" (Rev. 7:2), and occur when the first four angels blow their trumpets (Rev. 8).
>
> —*Be Victorious*, page 85

9. What are the challenges with a literal interpretation of the 144,000 Jews who are sealed? How is this passage an example of having only a "limited" human view of God's plan? Is it important to your faith that this section is literally true? Why or why not? What role does the Holy Spirit play in passages like this that can be somewhat unclear or potentially controversial in interpretation?

From the Commentary

> You cannot read the book of Revelation without develop-
> ing a global outlook, for the emphasis is on what God
> does for people in the *whole* world. The Lamb died to
> redeem people "out of every kindred, and tongue, and
> people, and nation" (Rev. 5:9). The great multitudes
> pictured here came from "all nations, and kindreds, and
> people, and tongues" (Rev. 7:9). "Go ye into all the world,
> and preach the gospel to every creature" was our Lord's
> mandate (Mark 16:15).
>
> There is no doubt as to who this multitude is, because
> one of the elders explained it to John (Rev. 7:14): They
> are Gentiles who have been saved through faith in Christ
> during the tribulation.... While today, in most parts of
> the world, it is relatively easy to confess Christ, this will
> not be the case during the tribulation, at least during the
> last half of it. Then, unless persons wear the "mark of the
> beast," they will not be able to buy or sell, and this would
> leave them without even life's bare necessities. Revelation
> 7:16 indicates that they suffered hunger (see Rev. 13:17),
> thirst (see Rev. 16:4), and lack of shelter. (On the heat of
> the sun, see Rev. 16:8–9.)
>
> —*Be Victorious*, page 87

10. Why do you suppose the salvation of people from all the different nations
and cultures matters to God? Why does the passage include reference to

people no longer hungering or thirsting? How does this picture of people coming through tribulation to worship affect you?

Looking Inward

Take a moment to reflect on all that you've explored thus far in this study of Revelation 4—7. Review your notes and answers and think about how each of these things matters in your life today.

Tips for Small Groups: To get the most out of this section, form pairs or trios and have group members take turns answering these questions. Be honest and as open as you can in this discussion, but most of all, be encouraging and supportive of others. Be sensitive to those who are going through particularly difficult times and don't press for people to speak if they're uncomfortable doing so.

11. What elements of Revelation 4—7 are most puzzling for you? Is it important for you to understand every detail of the symbolism? Why or why not? What do you do when you come across something you don't understand in Scripture? What would be a wise way to deal with the things you don't understand in Revelation (and elsewhere in the Bible)?

12. What was your reaction to the scene of worship in Revelation 5? How does this description of worship compare with your experience of worship? What can you glean from this picture of worship that might help you worship God better today?

13. What does it mean to you to be "sealed by the Holy Spirit"? How does this affect the way you live your faith out in daily life?

Going Forward

14. Think of one or two things that you have learned that you'd like to work on in the coming week. Remember that this is all about quality, not quantity. It's better to work on one specific area of life and do it well than to work on many and do poorly (or to be so overwhelmed that you simply don't try).

Do you want to go deeper into the study of the symbolism in Revelation? Do you want deepen your worship? Be specific. Go back through Revelation 4—7 and put a star next to the phrase or verse that is most encouraging to you. Consider memorizing this verse.

Real-Life Application Ideas: This section of Revelation includes a beautiful hymn of worship before the story turns to God's wrath and ultimate judgment. Worship can be a very encouraging experience, especially in the midst of great turmoil. Consider leading a small worship service with your family or small group just to encourage one another and praise God for His sovereignty. Include songs, Scripture reading, and moments of silence to simply sit in wonder of God's awesome power and perfect plan.

Seeking Help

15. Write a prayer below (or simply pray one in silence), inviting God to work on your mind and heart in those areas you've previously noted. Be honest about your desires and fears.

Notes for Small Groups:

- *Look for ways to put into practice the things you wrote in the Going Forward section. Talk with other group members about your ideas and commit to being accountable to one another.*

- *During the coming week, ask the Holy Spirit to continue to reveal truth to you from what you've read and studied.*

- *Before you start the next lesson, read Revelation 8—11. For more in-depth lesson preparation, read chapters 6 and 7, "Blow the Trumpets!" and "A Time for Testimony," in* Be Victorious.

Judgments and Testimony
(REVELATION 8—11)

Before you begin …
- *Pray for the Holy Spirit to reveal truth and wisdom as you go through this lesson.*
- *Read Revelation 8—11. This lesson references chapters 6 and 7 in* Be Victorious. *It will be helpful for you to have your Bible and a copy of the commentary available as you work through this lesson.*

Getting Started

From the Commentary

The seal judgments now over, the trumpet judgments are about to begin. These will be followed by the bowl (vial) judgments, culminating in the destruction of Babylon and Christ's return to earth.… Note that the trumpet and the bowl judgments touch on the same areas.

The trumpet judgments are released during the first half of the tribulation, and the bowl judgments during the last half, which is also called "the wrath of God" (Rev. 14:10; 15:7).

—*Be Victorious,* page 91

1. What are the judgments associated with the seven trumpets (Rev. 8—11)? Underline each one. How do these judgments differ from the scroll judgments?

More to Consider: In what ways do the trumpet judgments parallel the plagues that God sent on the land of Egypt? (See Exodus 7—11.)

2. Choose one verse or phrase from Revelation 8—11 that stands out to you. This could be something you're intrigued by, something that makes you uncomfortable, something that puzzles you, something that resonates with you, or just something you want to examine further. Write that here.

Going Deeper

From the Commentary

> The opening of the seventh seal, and the blowing of the first six trumpets, brought about three dramatic results.
>
> The first result is preparation (Rev. 8:1–6).
>
> This preparation involves two factors: silence (Rev. 8:1) and supplication (Rev. 8:2–6).
>
> The hosts in heaven had just worshipped the Father and the Lamb with a tremendous volume of praise (Rev. 7:10–12). But when the Lamb opened the seventh seal, heaven was silent for about thirty minutes. John does not tell us what caused the silence, but several possibilities exist. The scroll had now been opened completely, and perhaps even turned over, and all of heaven could see God's glorious plan unfolding.
>
> —*Be Victorious*, page 92

3. What do you think the silence after the seventh seal is opened symbolizes? In what way is this silence like the quiet before the storm? What role does supplication or prayer play during this preparation time? How might this kind of preparation be applicable to daily living?

From the Commentary

> The second result is desolation (Rev. 8:7–13).
>
> The first four trumpet judgments are "natural" in that they affect the land, the saltwater, the fresh water, and the heavenly bodies. The fifth and sixth judgments involve the release of demonic forces that first torment, and then kill. The last of the trumpet judgments (Rev. 11:15–19) creates a crisis among all the nations of the world.
>
> —*Be Victorious*, page 94

4. Circle the examples of desolation that occur with the first four trumpet judgments (Rev. 8:7–13). What stands out to you about these judgments? Why do you think the first trumpets signal earthly or "natural" aspects of the world?

From the Commentary

> The third result of the seventh seal is liberation (Rev. 9:1–21). The late Dr. Wilbur M. Smith, who made the book of Revelation his special study, once wrote: "It is

probable that, apart from the exact identification of Babylon in Revelation 17 and 18, the meaning of the two judgments in this chapter represents the most difficult major problem in the Revelation" (*Wycliffe Bible Commentary*, 1509). Revelation 9 describes two frightening armies that are liberated at just the right time and permitted to judge mankind.

(1) The army from the pit (vv. 1–12). The "bottomless pit" is literally "the pit of the abyss." Luke makes it clear that this "pit" is the abode of the demons (Luke 8:31), and John states that Satan will be temporarily "jailed" there during our Lord's reign on the earth (Rev. 20:1–3)....

(2) The army from the east (vv. 13–21). It was at the golden altar of incense that the angel offered the prayers of the saints (Rev. 8:3–5); now from this same altar a voice speaks, commanding that four angels be loosed. These angels are apparently wicked, because no holy angel would be bound. Each angel is in charge of part of the vast army that follows them at their liberation, an army of 200 million beings! The army is released at a precise time, for a special purpose: to kill (not just torment) a third of the world's population. Since a fourth of mankind has already been killed (Rev. 6:8), this means that *half of the world's population will be dead* by the time the sixth trumpet judgment is completed....

Things will not look bright for God's people during this middle stage of the prophetic journey, but they will still

be overcomers through the power of the King of Kings
and Lord of Lords!

—*Be Victorious*, pages 98, 100, 102

5. What seems to be the core message of Revelation 9? Why do you think
this part of the revelation is so dramatic? How might the early Christians
who were suffering persecution have received this?

From Today's World

Throughout modern history, there have been many proclamations that
we're living in the end times. While some of these conclusions have come
from the general state of our nation and world (wars, natural disasters, economic failures), some people have gone so far as to match events described
in Revelation directly to events in history. Some even have made claims
about the Antichrist, identifying him with a specific person.

6. Why do some Christians make bold claims about the end times?
What prompts believers to pursue this line of thinking? What value is
there in attempting to tie the message of Revelation directly to modern
circumstances? What are the dangers of doing this?

From the Commentary

> Revelation 10—14 describes the events that will occur at the middle of the seven-year tribulation. This explains John's repeated mention of the three-and-a-half-year time segment in one form or another (Rev. 11:2–3; 12:6, 14; 13:5). At the beginning of this period, the Antichrist began to make his conquest by promising to protect the Jews and assist in their rebuilding of the temple in Jerusalem. But after three-and-a-half years, he will break his agreement, invade the temple, and begin to persecute the Jewish people.
>
> —*Be Victorious*, page 105

7. Revelation features a lot of specific numbers and spans of times. Go through Revelation 10—11 and underline every number and mention of days or months. Why are there so many specific number references in what is often considered to be a mostly symbolic book? What does this tell us about God's intent for the revelation? What are Christians meant to get out of the specific numbers?

From the Commentary

However depressing the events of this middle segment of the tribulation may be, God is not without His witness to the world. In Revelation 10—11 are three important testimonies: from a mighty angel (Rev. 10:1–11), from the two special witnesses (Rev. 11:1–14), and from the elders in heaven (Rev. 11:15–19).

The testimony of the mighty angel is found in Revelation 10:1–11. More than sixty references to angels are made in Revelation. They are God's army sent to accomplish His purposes on earth. Believers today seldom think about these servants (Heb. 1:14), but one day in heaven we shall learn about all they did for us here.

This angel amazes us, for he has some of the characteristics that belong especially to the Lord Jesus Christ. John had seen and heard a "strong angel" (Rev. 5:2), and the same Greek word is here translated "mighty," All angels excel in strength (Ps. 103:20), but apparently some have greater power and authority than others.

—*Be Victorious*, pages 105–6

8. In what way are some of the characteristics of the mighty angel described in Revelation 10:1–11 similar to the characteristics of Jesus? Circle these. What's the purpose of Revelation 10? Why is it important that a "mighty angel" appears during this tribulation time? What does this tell us about the role of angels in the end times?

From the Commentary

> The testimony of the witnesses is found in Revelation 11:1–14. The place is Jerusalem and the time is the first half of the tribulation. Israel is worshipping again at its restored temple, built under the protection of the Antichrist, whose true character has not yet been revealed. To spiritualize Revelation 11:1–2 and make the temple refer to the church creates a number of serious problems. For one thing, how could John measure an invisible body of people, even if the church were still on earth? If the temple is the church, then who are the worshippers and what is the altar? And since the church unites Jews and Gentiles in one body (Eph. 2:11ff.), why are the Gentiles segregated in this temple? It seems wisest to interpret this temple as an actual building in the Holy City of Jerusalem (Neh. 11:1, 18; Dan. 9:24).

> —*Be Victorious*, page 109

9. How do you know when a passage of Scripture is literal and when it's symbolic or figurative? As you consider the details in Revelation 11, why might some people tend to see all of the content as figurative? What do we gain by making decisions about what each detail represents? What might we miss?

From the Commentary

The testimony of the elders is found in Revelation 11:15–19. We have been waiting since Revelation 8:13 for this third "woe" to arrive and now it is here. When the seventh angel blew the trumpet, three dramatic events occurred.

(1) An announcement of victory (v. 15).

(2) An acclamation of praise (vv. 16–18).

(3) An assurance of God's faithfulness (v. 19).

—*Be Victorious*, pages 113, 116

10. What message does Revelation 11:15–19 offer about God's ultimate plan for His people? How might this passage have been a comfort to those suffering persecution in John's day? How can it be a comfort for us today?

Looking Inward

Take a moment to reflect on all that you've explored thus far in this study of Revelation 8—11. Review your notes and answers and think about how each of these things matters in your life today.

Tips for Small Groups: To get the most out of this section, form pairs or trios and have group members take turns answering these questions. Be honest and as open as you can in this discussion, but most of all, be encouraging and supportive of others. Be sensitive to those who are going through particularly difficult times and don't press for people to speak if they're uncomfortable doing so.

11. Do any of the judgments noted in Revelation make you uncomfortable? If so, why? What can you take away personally from these bold descriptions of God's judgment?

12. When you consider the state of the world today, do you think we're in the end times prophesied in Revelation? Why or why not? How does your belief about these things affect your daily approach to pursuing a life of faith?

13. Much of the imagery in Revelation is vivid and violent. Why do you think God chose to use such imagery in this revelation? What does it say about God's coming judgment? About the people He knew would read these words? In what ways is this section of Revelation frightening to you? Encouraging?

Going Forward

14. Think of one or two things that you have learned that you'd like to work on in the coming week. Remember that this is all about quality, not quantity. It's better to work on one specific area of life and do it well than to work on many and do poorly (or to be so overwhelmed that you simply don't try).

Do you want to come to terms with God's role as the Judge of evil? Do you want to study the historical context for this section of Scripture?

Be specific. Go back through Revelation 8—11 and put a star next to the phrase or verse that is most encouraging to you. Consider memorizing this verse.

> *Real-Life Application Ideas: Though these chapters in Revelation include plenty of frightening content, the ultimate message is of God's victory. Set aside a day to consider and pray for all those in today's world who are suffering because of evil. Use this prayer time to ask for God's grace and comfort for those who are in pain, and hope for those who feel hopeless. Thank God for His ultimate victory over evil that is promised in Revelation. Also, in your prayer time, ask God to lead you to practical action you can take to spread the joy and good news of God's overcoming power.*

Seeking Help

15. Write a prayer below (or simply pray one in silence), inviting God to work on your mind and heart in those areas you've previously noted. Be honest about your desires and fears.

Notes for Small Groups:

- *Look for ways to put into practice the things you wrote in the Going Forward section. Talk with other group members about your ideas and commit to being accountable to one another.*

- *During the coming week, ask the Holy Spirit to continue to reveal truth to you from what you've read and studied.*

- *Before you start the next lesson, read Revelation 12—13. For more in-depth lesson preparation, read chapter 8, "The Terrible Trio," in* Be Victorious.

A Terrible Trio
(REVELATION 12—13)

Before you begin …
- *Pray for the Holy Spirit to reveal truth and wisdom as you go through this lesson.*
- *Read Revelation 12—13. This lesson references chapter 8 in* Be Victorious. *It will be helpful for you to have your Bible and a copy of the commentary available as you work through this lesson.*

Getting Started

From the Commentary

Revelation 12—13 introduces us to the three key characters in the drama of the last half of the tribulation: Satan the dragon, the false Christ, and the false prophet. These three are, in a sense, an evil trinity, opposing the true God and His people on earth. While these events will be of special significance to God's people at that time, the message of these two chapters can encourage suffering saints during any age.

God has permitted His people to suffer under the despotism of these rulers, but He has also enabled His people to experience great victories, even in martyrdom. They have been true overcomers! Then He has brought deliverance, only to have the cycle repeat itself, with each succeeding dictatorship worse than the previous one. The climax will come with the appearance of the Antichrist in his time (2 Thess. 2).

—*Be Victorious,* pages 121–22

1. Why does God allow His people to suffer during the last half of the tribulation as described in Revelation 12—13? Why wouldn't God simply choose to protect His people during this time? What does this tell us about God's plan? About God's people?

More to Consider: Many people believe that the "beast" noted in this section of Revelation is a future world dictator who promises to solve the pressing problems of the nations and that the false prophet is his "propaganda minister." Why would such a person be so compelling a figure? What warnings does this passage in Scripture offer us about trusting world leaders? What are the dangers of pushing this warning too far?

2. Choose one verse or phrase from Revelation 12—13 that stands out to you. This could be something you're intrigued by, something that makes you uncomfortable, something that puzzles you, something that resonates with you, or just something you want to examine further. Write that here.

Going Deeper

From the Commentary

John's vision opens with *two wonders in heaven* (Rev. 12:1–6). The first is a woman giving birth to a son. Since this child is identified as Jesus Christ (compare Rev. 12:5 with Rev. 19:15 and Ps. 2:9), this symbolic woman can be none other than the nation Israel. It was through Israel that Jesus Christ came into the world (Rom. 1:3; 9:4–5). By further comparing the description in Revelation 12:1 with Genesis 37:9–10, the identification seems certain.

In the Old Testament, Israel is often compared to a woman, and even a woman in travail (Isa. 54:5; 66:7; Jer.

3:6–10; Mic. 4:10; 5:2–3). The apostate world system is compared to a harlot (Rev. 17:1ff.), and the church to a pure bride (Rev. 19:7ff.).

The son is born and is then caught up to the throne of God (Rev. 12:5). We have symbolized here the birth of Christ and His victorious ascension, but nothing is said about either His life or His death. The colon in the middle of the verse represents thirty-three years of history!

The woman with child is the first wonder; the great red dragon is the second. Revelation 12:9 makes it clear that this is Satan.

—*Be Victorious*, pages 122–23

3. Review Revelation 12:7–8. What is the "war in heaven"? What does this entire chapter of Revelation reveal to us about spiritual warfare? Why is this important in the context of the end times? Why is this important in the context of daily living?

From the Commentary

Even today Satan has access to heaven, where he accuses God's people, but he cannot dethrone the exalted Savior. His strategy is to persecute God's people and devour them if possible (1 Peter 5:8). He has a special hatred for the Jewish people and has been the power behind anti-Semitism from the days of Pharaoh and Haman (see the book of Esther) to Hitler and Stalin. Finally, in the middle of the tribulation, there will come a wave of anti-Semitism such as the world has never seen (Rev. 12:6). But God will protect His people during those three-and-a-half years (1,260 days; see Rev. 11:2; 13:5).

Apart from the 144,000 (who are sealed and protected), a believing remnant of Jews will survive this very troublesome time. We are not told where God will protect them or who it is that will care for them. Matthew 24:15–21 will take on special meaning for those believing Jews who live in the end days. Note especially the parenthesis in Revelation 12:15.

—*Be Victorious*, pages 123–24

4. What does Revelation 12 teach us about Satan's plan? About his power? About his hatred for God's people?

From Today's World

The picture of Satan painted by modern society is one that falls far short of the evil character painted in the book of Revelation. Whether it's a movie's portrayal of Satan as a smarmy but clever lawyer or a cartoon's depiction of the now-familiar red-suited "devil" with horns and a tail, very little of Satan's true evil makes it into popular culture. Many people—including a large group of Christians—would prefer to believe that Satan is nothing more than a fictional character, someone who can act as an archetype of evil, but not someone who truly exists and is working diligently to thwart God's plan for the world.

5. Why do so many people deny the existence of Satan? How does popular media's portrayal of him influence our view of his role in this world? What are the dangers of not taking Satan seriously enough? Of focusing too much on Satan?

From the Commentary

The next scene in this cosmic drama is a *war in heaven* (Rev. 12:7–12). Scripture makes it clear that Satan has access to heaven even today (Job 1—2). Once he was the highest of God's angels, but he rebelled against God and was cast down (Isa. 14:12–15). Interestingly, as God's church faithfully serves Christ and wins the lost, Satan is also cast down and defeated (Luke 10:1–2, 17–20; Matt. 16:18; note also 12:29).

Of course, when Jesus Christ died on the cross, it meant Satan's ultimate defeat (John 12:31–33). Satan will one day be cast out of heaven (Rev. 12:7–10), and then finally cast into hell (Rev. 20:10).

What is this celestial conflict all about? The fact that Michael led God's angels to victory is significant, because Michael is identified with the nation Israel (Dan. 10:10–21; 12:1; note also Jude 9). The name *Michael* means "who is like God?" and this certainly parallels Satan's egocentric attack on Jehovah—"I will be like the Most High" (Isa. 14:14). Apparently, the Devil's hatred of Israel will spur him to make one final assault against the throne of God, but he will be defeated by Michael and a heavenly host.

But perhaps there is another factor involved in this war. After the church is taken to heaven, believers will stand before the judgment seat of Christ and have their works examined. On the basis of this judgment, rewards will be given (Rom. 14:10–12; 1 Cor. 3:10–15; 2 Cor. 5:10–11). It seems likely that Satan will be present at this event and will accuse the saints, pointing out all the "spots and wrinkles" in the church (Eph. 5:24–27).

—*Be Victorious*, pages 124–25

6. What is the warning in Revelation 12:12 all about? Why is the Devil furious in this passage? What does it mean that the Devil's time is short? Why might that be meaningful to Christians today?

From the Commentary

The sea symbolizes the Gentile nations (Rev. 17:15). From one of them, Satan will bring forth his "Super Leader," the man we call "Antichrist." Up to this point, the Antichrist has headed a ten-nation European league, but now he is about to embark on a new career as Satan's world dictator.

You will remember that the Antichrist began his career as a peacemaker (Rev. 6:2) and even "settled" the Arab-Israeli problem by making a covenant with the Jews to protect them for seven years (Dan. 9:27). This protection would permit the nation to rebuild the temple and rein-stitute religious rituals (Dan. 9:27; Rev. 11:1). But in the middle of the seven-year period (the time we are studying now in Rev. 10—14), he will break that covenant, stop the ceremonies, and set up himself as god in the temple (Dan. 9:27; 2 Thess. 2:1–12).

The symbolic description of "the beast" enables us to learn something about his origin and character. God does not see him as a man, made in the divine image, but as a wild animal, under the control of Satan. He is a man (Rev. 13:18), but he is energized from hell, for he comes out of the pit (Rev. 11:7; 17:8). Just as Jesus Christ is God in the flesh, so "the beast" will be Satan in a human body (see John 13:2, 27).

The seven heads represent seven mountains (Rev. 17:9), and since Rome was built on seven hills, this must be a veiled reference to that powerful city (see Rev. 17:18). It would be a most meaningful allusion in John's day!

The ten horns represent ten kingdoms (Dan. 7:24; Rev. 17:12). It appears that "the beast" will head a "United States of Europe," a revived Roman Empire, before taking over as world dictator. All nations will no doubt admire and thank him for the "peace" he has achieved, little realizing the sorrow and destruction he will bring to the world.

The three animals named in Revelation 13:2 remind us of the four beasts Daniel saw in his dream (Dan. 7): a lion (Babylon), a bear (Media-Persia), a leopard (Greece), and a "terrible beast" (the Antichrist). John saw these animals, or kingdoms, in reverse order since he was looking *back*, while Daniel was looking *ahead*. The final world empire will be rooted in all the previous empires and unite in one their evil and power. Added to the ferocity of these beasts will be Satan's own power, throne, and authority!

—*Be Victorious*, pages 127–28

7. Do you think our analysis of Revelation should influence our views on current political situations, such as the Middle East conflict and the European Union? If so, how? If not, why not?

From the Commentary

Once Satan presents his great "masterpiece," the counterfeit Christ, to the world, what will happen next?

First, there will be *wonder* (Rev. 13:3). Certainly a terrified world will wonder at the Antichrist's power and his sudden rise to international fame and authority....

Not only will there be wonder, but there will also be *worship* (Rev. 13:4). Worship is the one thing Satan has always wanted (Matt. 4:8–10), and he will receive it through "the beast." The second "beast," described in the last half of this chapter, will organize and promote the worship of the Antichrist, making it the official religion of the world!

There will also be *words* (Rev. 13:5–6). Almost all dictators have risen to power by controlling people with their words. Some of us can recall when Adolf Hitler was rising to power, and know now how he mesmerized huge crowds

with his speeches. Satan will make "the beast" a great ora-
tor, whose addresses will blaspheme God, His name, His
tabernacle (heaven), and the saints in heaven....

Finally, there will be *war* (Rev. 13:7–10). God will permit
the Antichrist to war against His people ("wear out the
saints," Dan. 7:25) and even to defeat some of them. John
prophesied that some of the saints will be captured and
some will be martyred. But because of their faith, they
will have patience, or endurance (see Heb. 6:12; Rev. 1:9),
and will not deny the Lord in spite of persecution and
death.

The world's population will be divided: Those who are
saved, with their names in God's book, will not submit
to "the beast"; those who are lost—the earth-dwellers—
will worship "the beast" and do his bidding. Note that
Revelation 13:9 applies this truth to "any man," no
matter in which age he may live. Certainly in John's day,
this was meaningful; for every Roman citizen had to
acknowledge, "Caesar is Lord." Likewise in every age of
the church, true believers have had to take their stand for
Christ, come what may.

—*Be Victorious*, pages 128–30

8. Read Job 1—2 and Luke 22:31–32, and consider the truths there in
light of Revelation 13. Why is it significant that Satan can do nothing
without God's permission? How does this apply to Revelation 13? Why
would God allow "the beast" such power? What does this tell us about how
God intends to work His ultimate plan?

More to Consider: Read John 5:43 and 2 Thessalonians 2:8–12. Why will the world accept the counterfeit Christ though it rejected Jesus? What does this suggest about the manner in which the counterfeit Christ will gain followers?

From the Commentary

In Revelation 16:13; 19:20; and 20:10, the beast from the earth is called "the false prophet." The dragon or Satan is the counterfeit Father ("I will be like the Most High"), "the beast" is the counterfeit Christ, and the false prophet is the counterfeit Holy Spirit. This completes the satanic trinity.

One of the ministries of the Holy Spirit is to glorify Christ and lead people to trust and worship Him (John 16:7–15). The false prophet will point to the Antichrist and his image and compel people to worship Satan through "the beast."

The image of the horns (Rev. 13:11) suggests that the false prophet has authority, but the absence of a crown indicates that his authority is not political. Our Lord warned that there would be false prophets (Matt. 24:11, 24), and this one will be the greatest. He will have the "character" of a lamb but the voice of the dragon.

—*Be Victorious*, page 131

9. What are the characteristics of the "false prophet" described in Revelation 13:11–18? What is significant about the "horns of a lamb" and "voice of a dragon" descriptors? What does that contrast suggest about the false prophet? About how he will appeal to the people?

From the Commentary

This special mark is the name or number of "the beast"— the mystical 666. In the ancient world, the letters of the alphabet were used for numbers, both in Greek and Hebrew, and Bible students have been attempting for years to unravel the mystery of this name and number. If you work at it hard enough, almost *any* name will fit!

Since man was created on the sixth day, six is the number of man. Creation was made for man and likewise has the number six stamped on it: twenty-four hours to a day (4 x 6), twelve months to a year (2 x 6). Seven is the number of perfection and fullness, but six is the "human number," just short of perfection.

Despite all man's imaginative calculations, we must confess that no one knows the meaning of this number and name. No doubt believers on earth at that time will understand it clearly. The "satanic trinity" cannot claim the number seven; it must settle for 666.

—*Be Victorious*, pages 132–33

10. Why are some Christians obsessed with the number of the beast? What are some of the ways numbers are used today that cause Christians to pause and ponder if they are related to the number of the beast? Apart from the curious and mysterious number itself, what is the main point of this passage about the number of the beast?

Looking Inward

Take a moment to reflect on all that you've explored thus far in this study of Revelation 12—13. Review your notes and answers and think about how each of these things matters in your life today.

Tips for Small Groups: To get the most out of this section, form pairs or trios and have group members take turns answering these questions. Be honest and as open as you can in this discussion, but most of all, be encouraging and supportive of others. Be sensitive to those who are going through particularly difficult times and don't press for people to speak if they're uncomfortable doing so.

11. When you think about the Antichrist, what image comes to mind? How has your church upbringing (or lack of it) affected your perception of the Antichrist and his role in the end times? What new insights have you gained about the Antichrist as you've studied these passages in Revelation?

12. How does the picture of the end times (so far) match with what you have been taught? Are you comforted by the prophecies? Frightened? Neither? Explain.

13. Have you ever been frightened when running into the number 666? Describe that time. Why does this number have such power over people? What fears does it put in you? What are some practical ways to be wary

of the number of the beast without overreacting to the number 666 in everyday life?

Going Forward

14. Think of one or two things that you have learned that you'd like to work on in the coming week. Remember that this is all about quality, not quantity. It's better to work on one specific area of life and do it well than to work on many and do poorly (or to be so overwhelmed that you simply don't try).

Do you want to better understand the role of the false prophet? Do you want to determine how to best prepare for the end times described in Revelation? Be specific. Go back through Revelation 12—13 and put a star next to the phrase or verse that is most encouraging to you. Consider memorizing this verse.

Real-Life Application Ideas: It's important to avoid overreacting to fears about the end-time events, but it's also valuable to develop a greater understanding about world events that may or may not have some bearing on these times. Make plans with your small group to explore other resources that offer opinions on current events and how they line up with end-time prophecies. As with any study, be open to discovering new things but also wary of proclamations that seem based on fear or questionable foundations. If nothing else, you will learn more about political systems and trends in the world today. Be sure to spend plenty of time in prayer for world leaders while you study these topics.

Seeking Help

15. Write a prayer below (or simply pray one in silence), inviting God to work on your mind and heart in those areas you've previously noted. Be honest about your desires and fears.

Notes for Small Groups:

- *Look for ways to put into practice the things you wrote in the Going Forward section. Talk with other group members about your ideas and commit to being accountable to one another.*

- *During the coming week, ask the Holy Spirit to continue to reveal truth to you from what you've read and studied.*

- *Before you start the next lesson, read Revelation 14—16. For more in-depth lesson preparation, read chapter 9, "Voices of Victory," in* Be Victorious.

Voices
(REVELATION 14—16)

Before you begin …
- *Pray for the Holy Spirit to reveal truth and wisdom as you go through this lesson.*
- *Read Revelation 14—16. This lesson references chapter 9 in* Be Victorious. *It will be helpful for you to have your Bible and a copy of the commentary available as you work through this lesson.*

Getting Started

From the Commentary

One of the themes that links Revelation 14—16 together is expressed by the word *voice*, which is used eleven times. In the events recorded, God speaks to His people or to the lost world, or His creatures speak out in praise of the Lord or in warning to the world. As the world moves into the last half of the tribulation, heaven is not silent.

—*Be Victorious,* page 137

1. Go through Revelation 14—16 and circle all the times the word *voice* is used. Why do you think this is such an important word for this section of Scripture? What does it tell us about the role of listening during times of trial and uncertainty?

2. Choose one verse or phrase from Revelation 14—16 that stands out to you. This could be something you're intrigued by, something that makes you uncomfortable, something that puzzles you, something that resonates with you, or just something you want to examine further. Write that here.

Going Deeper

From the Commentary

> This 144,000 is a special group of Jewish men who were
> sealed by God before the seventh seal was opened (Rev. 7),

and now they are seen on Mount Zion with the Lord Jesus Christ. Contrast this picture to the one described in Revelation 13: the followers of "the beast" whose mark is on their foreheads (Rev. 13:16). God always has His faithful people, no matter how wicked the world may become.

—*Be Victorious*, page 137

3. Review Revelation 14:1–5. God's chosen people are referenced many times in Scripture. What is significant about the mention of the 144,000 in this passage? What does this tell us about God's plan for these chosen people?

More to Consider: John pointed out that the 144,000 did not belong to the earth because they had been redeemed out of the earth. They were citizens of heaven. Read John 17:14–19 and Philippians 3:17–21. What are the implications of being citizens of heaven?

From the Commentary

At least six different angels are involved in the scene described in Revelation 14:6–20, each with a particular message to proclaim. Here are the first two messages:

(1) "Judgment is come" (vv. 6–7). During the present age, the angels are not privileged to preach the gospel. That responsibility has been given to God's people. While the nations will fear "the beast" and give honor to him, this heavenly messenger will summon them to fear and honor God alone. It is a reminder that God is the Creator and He alone deserves worship. This is not the gospel message as we know it (1 Cor. 15:1–4); rather, it is a return to the message of Romans 1:18ff., what theologians call "natural theology."

All creation bears witness to God's existence as well as to His power and wisdom. Nonetheless, "the beast" will convince men that he is in charge of the world, and that their destinies are in his hands....

(2) "Babylon is fallen" (v. 8). This proclamation anticipates the events of Revelation 18 (see also Rev. 16:18–19). We will consider it in detail then. "Babylon" is God's name for the world system of "the beast," the entire economic and political organization by which he rules. "The harlot" (Rev. 17) is the religious system that "the beast" uses to help build his organization. When the Antichrist establishes his own religion (Rev. 13:11–15), he

will destroy the "harlot," but it is God who will destroy Babylon.

—Be Victorious, page 139

4. Review Revelation 14:6–8. What is significant about the two proclamations in these verses? What judgment is coming, according to the first angel? What does the second angel mean that Babylon is "fallen"?

From the Commentary

Here are the third and fourth messages:

(3) "Escape God's wrath" (vv. 9–13). The third message is directed especially to those who are deciding about following "the beast." It is a warning that "the easy way" is really the hard way, that to "go along with the world" means to go away from God. The Greek text reads, "If any man continues to worship the beast," suggesting that there is still opportunity for repentance and salvation.…

(4) "The harvest is ripe" (vv. 14–20). The Person pictured here on the white cloud is undoubtedly our Lord

Jesus Christ (see Dan. 7:13–14; Rev. 1:13). We have had the image of the cup, and now we have the image of the harvest, both of the grain (Rev. 14:14–16) and of the grape (Rev. 14:17–20). Again, this anticipates the final judgment of the world.

—Be Victorious, pages 139–40

5. The third angel's proclamation suggests that many people will follow the beast. What sort of circumstances would need to be in place for such a beast to tempt people to follow him? What does this passage say about the challenges people will face in light of the compelling nature of the beast? What is the harvest that the angel refers to in Revelation 14:15–16?

From the Commentary

At this point, John saw the seven angels holding the seven vials of God's wrath, poised for action. The wicked world is about to "drink of the wine of the wrath of God" (Rev. 14:10), but before the angels pour out their judgments, there is an "interlude" of blessing. Before sending the "third woe" (Rev. 11:14), God once again reassures His faithful people.

John saw the believers from the tribulation who had overcome "the beast" and his system. These are the people who "loved not their lives unto the death" (Rev. 12:11). Since they did not cooperate with the satanic system and receive the mark of "the beast," they were unable to buy or sell (Rev. 13:17). They were totally dependent on the Lord for their daily bread. Some of them were put into prison and some were slain (Rev. 13:10), but all of them practiced faith and patience.

—*Be Victorious*, pages 141–42

6. Review Revelation 15:3–4. How is this song similar to the song of the Israelites after the exodus (Ex. 15)? Why is there a song of praise at this point in the story?

From the Commentary

In their song, the tribulation saints praise God's works as well as His ways. The earth-dwellers certainly would not praise God for His works, and they would never understand His ways. God's works are great and marvelous, and His ways are just and true. There is no complaint here about the way God permitted these people to suffer! It would save us a great deal of sorrow if we would acknowledge God's sovereignty in this same way today! "The Lord is righteous in all his ways, and holy in all his works" (Ps. 145:17).

The phrase "king of saints" can also be read "king of ages." God is the eternal King, but He is also in charge of history. Nothing happens by accident. The singers seek to glorify God and honor Him, the very praise the first angel proclaimed in Revelation 14:7. Antecedents of this song may be found in Psalms 86:9; 90:1–2; 92:5; 98:2; 111:9; and 145:17.

Revelation 15:4 is another anticipation of the kingdom, foretelling the time when all nations shall worship the Lamb and obey Him. This verse also announces that God's judgments are about to be manifested.

—*Be Victorious*, pages 142–43

7. What does Revelation 15 tell us about the resilience of people who overcome the beast? What does it say about the power of God to help people endure impossible circumstances? What does it teach us about the role and purpose of worship?

From the Commentary

> The "great voice" out of the temple commands the seven
> angels to pour out the contents of their vials (Rev. 16:1),
> after which he announces "It is done" (Rev. 16:17). The
> "mystery of God" is finished (Rev. 10:7)! The martyrs
> in glory had asked, "How long?" (Rev. 6:9–11) and now
> their cry would be answered.
>
> —*Be Victorious*, page 143

8. The phrase "It is done" (Rev. 16:17) is very similar to what Jesus said
upon the cross just before He died (John 19:30). How are the two uses
of the phrase similar? What does it mean that the "mystery of God" is
finished?

From the Commentary

> Each of the angels has a specific "target" for the contents
> of his vial. The earth-dwellers have already suffered from
> the seal and trumpet judgments, but this final series of

judgments will climax God's plan, leading to Babylon's fall and Jesus Christ's return to earth.

The first vial judgment (Rev. 16:2) of grievous sores reminds us of the sixth plague in Egypt (Ex. 9:8–12; note also Deut. 28:27, 35). Only those who have submitted to "the beast" and who have rejected the warning of the first angel will experience this judgment (Rev. 14:6–7)....

The second and third vials parallel the first plague in Egypt (Ex. 7:14–25). The second vial will center on the sea, and the third will turn the inland waters (rivers and fountains) into blood....

All earthly life depends on the light of the sun. In previous judgments, a part of the sun had been dimmed (Rev. 8:12), but now with the fourth vial judgment, the heat of the sun is increased. Anyone who has been in the desert knows how merciless the sun's heat can be. Remembering too that the water system is now useless, you can imagine how people will suffer from thirst. Alas, even this judgment will not bring men to their knees (see Mal. 4:1)!

The darkness referred to in Revelation 16:10–11 is not worldwide darkness; only "the beast," his throne, and his kingdom are affected. This reminds us of the fifth trumpet (Rev. 9:2) and the ninth plague (Ex. 10:21–23)....

When God sent the ninth plague to Egypt, the entire land was dark, except for Goshen where the Israelites lived. The judgment of the fifth vial is just the opposite: There is light for the world, but darkness reigns at the headquarters of "the beast"! Certainly this will be a great blow to his "image" throughout the earth.

With the sixth vial, the Euphrates dries up (Rev. 16:12–16). This famous river was mentioned earlier in Revelation, when the sixth trumpet sounded (Rev. 9:13ff.) and the angels were loosed who were bound therein. At that time, an army of demonic horsemen was also released. Now, an army from the nations of the world gathers for the great battle at Armageddon. The drying up of the river will make it possible for the army of the "kings of the East" to come to Palestine and invade the Holy Land.

—*Be Victorious*, pages 143–45

9. What are the justifications for each of the vial judgments? Why again is there such similarity between these judgments and the previous ones, as well as the plagues that God sent during the exodus? How might the familiarity of these kinds of events have been received by the original audience for John's revelation? Why is it significant to Christians today?

More to Consider: The name Armageddon *comes from two Hebrew words,* har Megiddo, *the hill of Megiddo. The word* Megiddo *means "place of troops" or "place of slaughter." It is also called the Plain of Esdraelon and the Valley of Jezreel. The area is about fourteen miles wide and twenty miles long and forms what Napoleon called "the most natural battlefield of the whole earth." As you consider the origin of the word* Armageddon, *why is it an appropriate term for the battle referenced in Revelation?*

From the Commentary

Reviewing Revelation 14—16, we see the encouragement they give to suffering Christians. The sealed 144,000 will arrive on Mount Zion and praise God (Rev. 14:1–5). The martyrs will also be in glory, praising God (Rev. 15:1–4). John's message is clear: It is possible to be victorious over "the beast" and be an overcomer!

Movements of armies, confederations of nations, and worldwide opposition to God cannot hinder the Lord from fulfilling His Word and achieving His purposes. Men think they are free to do as they please, but in reality, they are accomplishing the plans and purposes of God!

Every generation of Christians has been able to identify with the events in Revelation 14—16. There has always been a "beast" to oppress God's people and a false prophet to try to lead them astray. We have always been on the verge of an "Armageddon" as the nations wage war.

But in the last days, these events will accelerate and the Bible's prophecies will be ultimately fulfilled. I believe the church will not be on the scene at that time, but both Jewish and Gentile believers will be living who will have to endure the Antichrist's rule.

—*Be Victorious*, page 148

10. What are some ways Christians over the past few decades have been able to relate to the events in Revelation 14—16? What are some of the "beasts" that have oppressed God's people? Who are some of the false prophets Christianity has encountered? What encouragement does this entire section of Revelation give to us about God's role in the lives of people who are suffering from persecution and oppression?

Looking Inward

Take a moment to reflect on all that you've explored thus far in this study of Revelation 14—16. Review your notes and answers and think about how each of these things matters in your life today.

Tips for Small Groups: To get the most out of this section, form pairs or trios and have group members take turns answering these questions. Be honest and as open as you can in this discussion, but most of all, be encouraging and supportive of others. Be sensitive to those who are going through particularly difficult times and don't press for people to speak if they're uncomfortable doing so.

11. What do you think the "mark of the beast" will be? Are you afraid of the "mark of the beast"? Why or why not?

12. What is your reaction to the judgments proclaimed by the seven angels? What does this tell you about God? Do these acts of God cause you to respect Him? Worship Him? Fear Him? What do you think God wants you to glean from this section of Scripture?

13. What are some of the ways you've been oppressed as a believer? How do they compare with the kinds of oppression described in Revelation? How can this passage of Scripture give you hope in the midst of oppression or spiritual warfare?

Going Forward

14. Think of one or two things that you have learned that you'd like to work on in the coming week. Remember that this is all about quality, not quantity. It's better to work on one specific area of life and do it well than to work on many and do poorly (or to be so overwhelmed that you simply don't try).

Do you want to have more courage when you face opposition to living as a Christian? Be specific. Go back through Revelation 14—16 and put a star next to the phrase or verse that is most encouraging to you. Consider memorizing this verse.

Real-Life Application Ideas: Since the theme of Revelation is "overcomers," make a list of people you know who have demonstrated this ability to overcome great obstacles and challenges. Interview one or two to discover how they endured in the face of trials and tribulations. Collect all the practical wisdom you can from these interviews, then apply it to any challenges you might be facing in life.

Seeking Help

15. Write a prayer below (or simply pray one in silence), inviting God to work on your mind and heart in those areas you've previously noted. Be honest about your desires and fears.

Notes for Small Groups:

- *Look for ways to put into practice the things you wrote in the Going Forward section. Talk with other group members about your ideas and commit to being accountable to one another.*

- *During the coming week, ask the Holy Spirit to continue to reveal truth to you from what you've read and studied.*

- *Before you start the next lesson, read Revelation 17—18. For more in-depth lesson preparation, read chapter 10, "Desolation and Destruction!" in* Be Victorious.

Destruction
(REVELATION 17—18)

Before you begin …
- *Pray for the Holy Spirit to reveal truth and wisdom as you go through this lesson.*
- *Read Revelation 17—18. This lesson references chapter 10 in* Be Victorious. *It will be helpful for you to have your Bible and a copy of the commentary available as you work through this lesson.*

Getting Started

From the Commentary

Beginning in Revelation 17, John describes the Lamb's step-by-step victory over "the beast" and his kingdom. In Revelation 17, the religious system is judged; in Revelation 18, the political and economic systems fall victim. Finally, the Lord Himself returns to earth; judges Satan, "the beast," and the false prophet (Rev. 19:19–20); and then establishes His kingdom.

—*Be Victorious*, page 151

1. Why is it important to have the detailed descriptions of the Lamb's victory over the beast and his kingdom? What is the value of wrestling with the details here? What is the purpose of the symbolism used throughout this section of Revelation? Who is it intended for?

More to Consider: Every age has featured a "Babylon," a political and economic system that has sought to control people's minds and destinies. What are some of the "Babylons" people have encountered throughout history? Are there any today? What are the clues that lead you to believe these systems may be evil and controlling?

2. Choose one verse or phrase from Revelation 17—18 that stands out to you. This could be something you're intrigued by, something that makes you uncomfortable, something that puzzles you, something that resonates with you, or just something you want to examine further. Write that here.

Going Deeper

From the Commentary

> In Revelation 17 and 18, John prophesies two divine judgments. The first is the desolation of the harlot.
>
> The scene begins with *an invitation* (Rev. 17:1–2). One of the angels asks John to come and see what God will do with "the beast's" worldwide religious system. Four times in this chapter, the woman is called a "harlot" (Rev. 17:1, 5, 15–16), and her sin is called "fornication" (Rev. 17:2, 4). Her evil influence has extended to the whole world, reaching even into high places ("the kings of the earth").
>
> —*Be Victorious*, pages 151–52

3. Why do you think John was astonished (Rev. 17:6)? Who is the "harlot"? Why would God use the word *harlot* in this context? What implications might that have had to the early Christians reading this revelation for the first time? Why is the word *fornication* appropriate to describe the "harlot's" sin?

From the Commentary

> John's readers would not be surprised when he used an
> evil harlot to symbolize a wicked city or political system.
> God even called Jerusalem a harlot (Isa. 1:21). Isaiah said
> that Tyre was a harlot (Isa. 23:16–17), and Nahum used
> this same designation for Nineveh (Nah. 3:4).
>
> —*Be Victorious*, page 153

4. Read Jeremiah 50—51. What parallels can you draw from this passage
to John's prophetic message?

From the Commentary

> Readers in John's day would identify "the harlot" with
> the Roman Empire. Readers in the Middle Ages might
> identify it as the Roman ecclesiastical system. Today,
> some believers see "the harlot" and the Babylonian system
> in an apostate "world church" that minimizes doctrinal
> truth, rejects the authority of the Word, and tries to unite

professed believers on some other basis than faith in Jesus Christ.

However, in the days when John's prophecy will be fulfilled, an amazing thing will happen: "The harlot" will be made desolate by the very system that carried her! It is important to note that *"the beast" carries "the harlot."* Satan (and the Antichrist) will use the apostate religious system to accomplish his own ends (i.e., attain world power), but then he will do away with "the harlot" and establish his own religious system. And all of this will be the fulfillment of God's Word (Rev. 17:17).

—*Be Victorious*, page 155

5. Revelation 17 includes more vivid imagery in its description of the desolation. What is the purpose of such gruesome imagery? Why do you think God chose to describe the victory over the beast with such detail?

From the Commentary

Satan's counterfeit religion is subtle, requiring spiritual discernment to recognize. It was Paul's great concern that the local churches he founded not be seduced away from their sincere devotion to Christ (2 Cor. 11:1–4). In every age, there is the tremendous pressure to conform to "popular religion" and to abandon the fundamentals of the faith. In these last days, we all need to heed the admonitions in 1 Timothy 4 and 2 Timothy 3 and remain true to our Lord.

—*Be Victorious*, page 156

6. Review 1 Timothy 4 and 2 Timothy 3. What are the admonitions there that can help us avoid the counterfeit religion Satan offers? What are some of the subtle ways this counterfeit religion attacks Christianity? Why would Satan choose a subtle approach?

From the Commentary

Babylon was not only an ancient city and a powerful empire, but also the symbol of mankind's rebellion against God. In Revelation 18, Babylon represents the world system of "the beast," particularly in its economic and political aspects. At the same time, John calls Babylon a "city" at

least eight times (Rev. 14:8; 17:18; 18:10, 16, 18–21). Old
Testament prophecy seems to make clear that the city itself
will not be rebuilt (Isa. 13:19–22; Jer. 51:24–26, 61–64).
Some equate Babylon with Rome, particularly since "the
harlot" and "the beast" cooperate during the first half of
the tribulation. Perhaps Peter was using *Babylon* as a "code
name" for Rome when he wrote his first letter (1 Peter
5:13). Certainly, John's readers would think of the Roman
Empire as they read these words about Babylon.

—*Be Victorious*, page 156

7. Why would the fall of Babylon be viewed as an event worth celebrating
to the Christians who first heard John's revelation? How might they see
this prophecy in relation to their current crisis of persecution? How can we
apply the truths in this prophecy to our own challenging circumstances?

From the Commentary

John heard four voices give four important announce-
ments.

The first was the voice of condemnation (Rev. 18:1–3).

This announcement was anticipated in Revelation 14:8....
There is a definite reference here to Jeremiah 51—52,
where the prophet saw the fall of historical Babylon. But
here John saw the destruction of spiritual Babylon, the
world system organized by "the beast." It was no ordinary
angel that made this announcement, for he had great
power and a glory that radiated throughout the whole
earth. Despite Satan's devices and the opposition of evil
men, "the earth shall be filled with the knowledge of the
glory of the Lord" (Hab. 2:14).

—*Be Victorious*, pages 156–57

8. Why does the angel shout the proclamation in Revelation 18:1–3 with a
mighty voice? Why are these words so important?

More to Consider: Read 1 John 2:15–17. How is this warning applicable to those who are tempted by what the world system— "Babylon" in this context—has to offer?

From the Commentary

The second voice is a voice of separation (Rev. 18:4–8). This admonition parallels Jeremiah 50:8 and 51:6, 45. In all ages, God's true people have had to separate themselves from that which is worldly and anti-God. When God called Abraham, He ordered him to get out of his country (Gen. 12:1). God separated the Jewish nation from Egypt and warned the Israelites not to go back. The church today is commanded to separate itself from that which is ungodly (Rom. 16:17–18; 2 Cor. 6:14—7:1).

The third voice is the voice of lamentation (Rev. 18:9–19). This long paragraph describes the mourning of the merchants as they see Babylon go up in smoke and all their wealth destroyed. The image here is that of a prosperous ancient city that is visited by many ships. The wealth of the city provides for many nations and employs many people. It is worth noting that not only do the merchants lament the fall of Babylon (Rev. 18:11) but also the kings of the earth (Rev. 18:9). Business and government are so intertwined that what affects one affects the other.

—*Be Victorious*, pages 158–59

9. What does it mean to live "separate" lives as Christians today? How can we do this and still fulfill the Great Commission to preach the gospel? What is the message inherent in the voice of lamentation (Rev. 18:9–19)? How is this particularly apropos for today's culture of prosperity?

From the Commentary

> The fourth voice is a voice of celebration (Rev. 18:20–24). In contrast to the lament of the kings and merchants is the rejoicing of heaven's inhabitants that Babylon has fallen. How important it is that God's people look at events from God's point of view. In fact, we are commanded to rejoice at the overthrow of Babylon, because in this judgment God will vindicate His servants who were martyred (see Rev. 6:9–11).
>
> —*Be Victorious*, page 161

10. How are we supposed to celebrate the fall of Babylon? How is this different than being glad that sinners are being judged? Why does justice prompt a joyful response?

Looking Inward

Take a moment to reflect on all that you've explored thus far in this study of Revelation 17—18. Review your notes and answers and think about how each of these things matters in your life today.

Tips for Small Groups: To get the most out of this section, form pairs or trios and have group members take turns answering these questions. Be honest and as open as you can in this discussion, but most of all, be encouraging and supportive of others. Be sensitive to those who are going through particularly difficult times and don't press for people to speak if they're uncomfortable doing so.

11. Once again there is a lot of vivid imagery in these chapters. What imagery in Revelation 17—18 has the most emotional impact on you? Why do you think it has the most impact? What can you learn about yourself and your faith from the way you react to this content?

12. What are examples you've encountered of a "world church" that minimizes doctrinal truth or rejects the authority of the Word? Why is this sort of teaching often under the banner of uniting believers? Have you

been tempted to pursue this line of thinking? Why or why not? What are some things you do to keep anchored to doctrinal truth?

13. In what ways are you living a separate life, as the voice calls people to do in Revelation 18:4–8? In what ways are you tempted to pursue the ways of the world? What warnings does Revelation give about following these temptations?

Going Forward

14. Think of one or two things that you have learned that you'd like to work on in the coming week. Remember that this is all about quality, not quantity. It's better to work on one specific area of life and do it well than to work on many and do poorly (or to be so overwhelmed that you simply don't try).

Do you want to address the ways you are drawn to the world's value of possessions, entertainment, or applause? Be specific. Go back through Revelation 17—18 and put a star next to the phrase or verse that is most encouraging to you. Consider memorizing this verse.

Real-Life Application Ideas: One of the challenges that Christians will face in the end times is sorting through the many different voices claiming to be speaking the "truth." The best way to be prepared for combating a false doctrine is to be certain of the true doctrine of Christ. Working with a church leader or seasoned Christian friend, put together a document that outlines what you believe. Include any absolutes—the things that make up the foundation of your faith— and negotiables—the things you're still trying to understand but that don't affect the foundation of your faith should you encounter new wisdom that changes your mind. Refer to this document often, refining it as your faith grows. This way, you'll be ready to defend your beliefs and deflect false doctrine as you encounter it.

Seeking Help

15. Write a prayer below (or simply pray one in silence), inviting God to work on your mind and heart in those areas you've previously noted. Be honest about your desires and fears.

Notes for Small Groups:

- *Look for ways to put into practice the things you wrote in the Going Forward section. Talk with other group members about your ideas and commit to being accountable to one another.*

- *During the coming week, ask the Holy Spirit to continue to reveal truth to you from what you've read and studied.*

- *Before you start the next lesson, read Revelation 19—22. For more in-depth lesson preparation, read chapters 11 and 12, "The King and His Kingdom" and "All Things New!" in* Be Victorious.

The Kingdom
(REVELATION 19—22)

Before you begin ...
- *Pray for the Holy Spirit to reveal truth and wisdom as you go through this lesson.*
- *Read Revelation 19—22. This lesson references chapters 11 and 12 in* Be Victorious. *It will be helpful for you to have your Bible and a copy of the commentary available as you work through this lesson.*

Getting Started
From the Commentary

"How will it all end?" has been mankind's major question for centuries. Historians have studied the past, hoping to find a clue to understanding the future. Philosophers have tried to penetrate the meaning of things, but they have yet to find the key. No wonder perplexed people have turned in desperation to astrology and spiritism!

The prophetic Word of God shines like a "light ... in a

128 \ The Wiersbe Bible Study Series: Revelation

dark place" (2 Peter 1:19), and on that we can depend. Here in Revelation 19—20, John has recorded five key events that will take place before God "wraps up" human history and ushers in His new heavens and earth.

—*Be Victorious*, page 165

1. What are the five events noted in the previous commentary excerpt? (See these sections of Revelation: 19:1–10; 19:11—20:3; 20:4–6; 20:7–10; and 20:11–15.) Why are people so consumed by trying to understand the future? In what ways does Revelation shine like a light in a dark place? In what ways does it appear murky to believers? What role does faith play in our attempt to understand the meaning of Revelation?

2. Choose one verse or phrase from Revelation 19—22 that stands out to you. This could be something you're intrigued by, something that makes you uncomfortable, something that puzzles you, something that resonates with you, or just something you want to examine further. Write that here.

Going Deeper

From the Commentary

> Since the "great whore [harlot]" of Revelation 17 was destroyed by "the beast" and his fellow rulers (Rev. 17:16) in the middle of the tribulation, the "great whore" referred to here must be Babylon the Great. Comparing Revelation 17:2 with 18:3 and 9, the connection is obvious. Both the apostate religious system and the satanic economic-political system led the world astray and polluted mankind. Both were guilty of persecuting God's people and martyring many of them.
>
> The song emphasizes God's attributes, which is the proper way to honor Him. We do not rejoice at the sinfulness of Babylon, or even the greatness of Babylon's fall. We rejoice that God is "true and righteous" (Rev. 15:3; 16:7; 17:6) and that He is glorified by His holy judgments.
>
> —*Be Victorious*, pages 165–66

3. In what ways does the song in Revelation 19:1–4 emphasize God's attributes? What does this teach us about how to honor Him? (See Rev. 15:3; 16:7; 19:6.)

More to Consider: John was so overwhelmed by all of this that he fell down to worship the angel who was guiding him, an act that he later repeated (Rev. 22:8–9)! Of course, worshipping angels is wrong (Col. 2:18), and John knew this. We must take into account the tremendous emotional content of John's experience. How is John's response similar to the response some Christians have today to great speakers or teachers of God's truth? What does this tell us about the power (and danger) of our emotions in the context of our faith story?

From the Commentary

When Babylon fell on the earth, the command was given in heaven, "Rejoice over her!" (Rev. 18:20), and what we read in this section is heaven's response to that command. The word *alleluia* is the Greek form of the Hebrew word *hallelujah*, which means "praise the Lord." …

First, John described the Conqueror (Rev. 19:11–16) and then His conquests (Rev. 19:17—20:3). The rider on the white horse (Rev. 6:2) is the false Christ, but this Rider is the true Christ. He is not coming *in the air* to take His people home (1 Thess. 4:13–18), but *to the earth* with His people, to conquer His enemies and establish His kingdom.

—*Be Victorious*, pages 165, 68

4. Why does John describe the Conqueror as a rider on a white horse (19:11), when earlier the false Christ was referred to as a rider on a white horse? (See

Rev. 6:2.) How does this reframing of the "white horse" imagery make the message of God's victory even more dramatic? What does this tell us about the symbols that fill the entire book of Revelation?

From the Commentary

> The phrase "thousand years" occurs six times in Revelation 20:1–7. This period in history is known as "the millennium," from two Latin words, *mille* ("thousand") and *annum* ("year")—the 1,000-year kingdom of Christ on earth. At last, Christ and His church will reign over the nations of the earth, and Israel will enjoy the blessings promised by the prophets (see Isa. 2:1–5; 4:1–6; 11:1–9; 12:1–6; 30:18–26; 35:1–10)....
>
> At the close of the millennium, Satan will be released from the pit and permitted to lead one last revolt against the Lord. Why? As final proof that the heart of man is desperately wicked and can be changed only by God's grace. Imagine the tragedy of this revolt: People who have been living in a perfect environment, under the perfect government of God's Son, will finally admit the truth and rebel

against the King! Their obedience will be seen as mere *feigned* submission, and not true faith in Christ at all.

—*Be Victorious*, pages 171–74

5. What does this section of Revelation teach us about God's kingdom on earth? What message is God trying to teach us with the description of a time when Satan is permitted one last revolt? What does this say about the heart of man?

From the Commentary

There shall be a second resurrection, and the unsaved will be raised and will stand before God's judgment. Do not confuse this judgment at the White Throne with the judgment seat of Christ, where believers will have their works judged and rewarded. At this judgment, there will be only unbelievers, and there will be no rewards. John described here an awesome scene. Heaven and earth will flee away and no place will be left for sinners to hide! All must face the Judge!

—*Be Victorious*, page 174

6. Why is this second resurrection mentioned in John's revelation? What does this event tell us about God's judgment? Why is this important to understand in the context of God's ultimate plan for salvation?

From the Commentary

> Human history begins in a garden and ends in a city that is like a garden paradise. In the apostle John's day, Rome was the admired city, yet God compared it to a harlot. "That which is highly esteemed among men is abomination in the sight of God" (Luke 16:15). The eternal city of God is compared to a beautiful bride (Rev. 21:9), because it is the eternal home for God's beloved people.
>
> —*Be Victorious*, page 179

7. How is Revelation 21:5–6 a summary of the final two chapters of the book? In what ways does Revelation describe the completion of what began in Genesis?

From the Commentary

In Revelation 21, John gives us a threefold description of the citizens of the [garden-paradise] city.

(1) They are God's people (vv. 1–5). The first heaven and earth were prepared for the first man and woman and their descendants. God had readied everything for them when He placed them in the garden. Unfortunately, our first parents sinned, ushering death and decay into God's beautiful world. Creation is in bondage and travail (Rom. 8:18–23), and even the heavens "are not clean in His sight" (Job 15:15).

(2) The citizens of heaven are a satisfied people (v. 6). People who live in modern cities do not think much about water, but this was a major concern in John's day. No doubt John himself, working in the Roman mines, had known the meaning of thirst. Tortured saints throughout the ages would certainly identify with this wonderful promise from the Lord. Free and abundant living water for all!

(3) These heavenly citizens are an overcoming people (vv. 7–8). "He that overcometh" is a key phrase in this book (Rev. 2:7, 11, 17, 26; 3:5, 12, 21; note also 12:11). As John pointed out in his first epistle, all true believers are overcomers (1 John 5:4–5), so this promise is not just for the "spiritually elite." Because we are the children of God, we shall inherit all things.

—*Be Victorious*, pages 179–81

8. How does the description of this city compare with the description of the garden of Eden? How does it compare with the living conditions all humans have endured between the garden and the final resurrection?

From the Commentary

> The eternal city is not only the home of the bride; it *is* the bride! A city is not buildings; it is people. The city John saw was holy and heavenly; in fact, it descended to earth from heaven, where it was prepared. John's description staggers the imagination, even accepting the fact that a great deal of symbolism is involved. Heaven is a real place of glory and beauty, the perfect home for the Lamb's bride.
>
> —*Be Victorious*, page 182

9. Review Revelation 21:9—22:5. How does John describe the character of the city? Why do you think the revelation focuses on these particular elements? How would they have been significant to the early Christian culture? What can we take away from the description of the city that speaks

to us today? Is it important to understand all the details of the city? Why or why not? How does this section of Scripture offer Christians hope today?

More to Consider: What will we do in heaven for all eternity? Certainly, we shall praise the Lord, but we shall also serve Him (Rev. 22:3). How will serving the Lord in heaven differ from the way we serve Him on earth?

From the Commentary

Heaven is more than a destination; it is a motivation. Knowing that we shall dwell in the heavenly city ought to make a difference in our lives here and now. The vision of the heavenly city motivated the patriarchs as they walked with God and served Him (Heb. 11:10, 13–16). Knowing that He was returning to the Father in heaven also encouraged Jesus Christ as He faced the cross (Heb. 12:2). The assurance of heaven must not lull us into complacency or carelessness, but spur us to fulfill our spiritual duties.

—*Be Victorious*, page 186

10. What does this passage tell us we ought to be doing in order to prepare for heaven? In what ways is our participation in God's kingdom on earth part of that preparation? What does it mean to participate in God's kingdom on earth?

Looking Inward

Take a moment to reflect on all that you've explored thus far in this study of Revelation 19—22. Review your notes and answers and think about how each of these things matters in your life today.

Tips for Small Groups: To get the most out of this section, form pairs or trios and have group members take turns answering these questions. Be honest and as open as you can in this discussion, but most of all, be encouraging and supportive of others. Be sensitive to those who are going through particularly difficult times and don't press for people to speak if they're uncomfortable doing so.

11. Do you spend much time pondering the end of the world? Why or why not? What are the biggest questions you have about how things will end? Do these questions affect the way you live your daily life? If so, how?

12. What are your personal thoughts about the millennium alluded to in Revelation 20? How important is it to you that your beliefs about the end times are correct? How might this affect the manner in which you share your faith with others?

13. What are you most looking forward to about heaven? Do you live your life today in anticipation of heaven? In what ways are you living as part of God's kingdom on earth? Why is this important if the ultimate destination is heaven?

Going Forward

14. Think of one or two things that you have learned that you'd like to work on in the coming week. Remember that this is all about quality, not quantity. It's better to work on one specific area of life and do it well than to work on many and do poorly (or to be so overwhelmed that you simply don't try).

Do you want to live a more Christlike life now in light of your ultimate destiny? Be specific. Go back through Revelation 19—22 and put a star next to the phrase or verse that is most encouraging to you. Consider memorizing this verse.

Real-Life Application Ideas: One of the more common approaches to evangelism is to present the promise of heaven and allow the appeal of "a better life, forever" to compel people to accept Christ. However, this approach tends to put too much emphasis on the "not yet" part of living for Christ. With your small-group members or family, come up with an approach to sharing your faith that not only presents the wonderful promise of heaven but the promise of a better, richer life on earth as well—a kingdom life. Then look for opportunities to share this truth with friends and neighbors and coworkers. Don't sugarcoat the truth—a life of faith isn't all buttercups and butterflies. But speak from your own story about how God's love and nearness have helped you to live a meaningful life. And heaven? That's just the cherry on top of the ice cream!

Seeking Help

15. Write a prayer below (or simply pray one in silence), inviting God to work on your mind and heart in those areas you've previously noted. Be honest about your desires and fears.

Notes for Small Groups:

- Look for ways to put into practice the things you wrote in the Going Forward section. Talk with other group members about your ideas and commit to being accountable to one another.
- During the coming week, ask the Holy Spirit to continue to reveal truth to you from what you've read and studied.

Summary and Review

Notes for Small Groups: This session is a summary and review of this book. Because of that, it is shorter than the previous lessons. If you are using this in a small-group setting, consider combining this lesson with a time of fellowship or a shared meal.

> *Before you begin …*
> - *Pray for the Holy Spirit to reveal truth and wisdom as you go through this lesson.*
> - *Briefly review the notes you made in the previous sessions. You will refer back to previous sections throughout this bonus lesson.*

Looking Back

1. Over the past eight lessons, you've examined the book of Revelation. What expectations did you bring to this study? In what ways were those expectations met?

2. What is the most significant personal discovery you've made from this study?

3. What surprised you most about the prophecies (in particular, the specific imagery) in Revelation? What, if anything, troubled you?

Progress Report

4. Take a few moments to review the Going Forward sections of the previous lessons. How would you rate your progress for each of the things you chose to work on? What adjustments, if any, do you need to make to continue on the path toward spiritual maturity?

5. In what ways have you grown closer to Christ during this study? Take a moment to celebrate those things. Then think of areas where you feel you still need to grow and note those here. Make plans to revisit this study in a few weeks to review your growing faith.

Things to Pray About

6. Revelation is a book packed with symbolism, but it is also loaded with rich theology. As you reflect on John's revelation, ask God to reveal to you those truths that you most need to hear. Revisit the book often and seek the Holy Spirit's guidance to gain a better understanding of what it means to be an overcomer.

7. The messages in Revelation focus on truth, the dangers of deception, spiritual warfare, and the ultimate victory in Christ. Spend time praying about these topics.

8. Whether you've been studying this in a small group or on your own, there are many other Christians working through the very same issues you discovered when examining the book of Revelation. Take time to pray for each of them, that God would reveal truth, that the Holy Spirit would guide you, and that each person might grow in spiritual maturity according to God's will.

A Blessing of Encouragement

Studying the Bible is one of the best ways to learn how to be more like Christ. Thanks for taking this step. In closing, let this blessing precede you and follow you into the next week while you continue to marinate in God's Word:

May God light your path to greater understanding as you review the truths found in the book of Revelation and consider how they can help you grow closer to Christ.